GET PICKED

PRAISE FOR GET PICKED

"If you know your stuff, you should be on stage. People believe people on stage. But how to get there? How...to get picked? Read this book."

—Peter Shankman,
Corporate Keynote Speaker,
Founder: ShankMinds Business Masterminds

"Speaking at conferences is, hands down, the best way to raise your profile, be seen as an expert, and win business. Rather than focusing on one-to-one marketing methods, you can leverage your time by speaking to hundreds of prospects at once (usually, for free!). *Get Picked* is the book I wish I had written on the topic. Grab this fluff-free guide to getting your name in conference programs and implement the savvy advice today. Your business or career will thank you."

—Lori Nash Byron,
CEO, Famous in Your Field

"If you're working to become your best self and put out your best work, then you owe it to yourself—and the world—to share what you know with an audience. If that's through speaking, *Get Picked* is the book you need. Learn how to find an audience and how to pitch topics that will get you selected to speak at conferences and industry events. Don't hide what you know, take action, and start taking action by buying this book!"

- Kelsey Humphreys,
Host of "The Pursuit" and Bestselling Author of *Go Solo*

"Thought leadership is a prized commodity in today's content-focused world. And David and Aurora really understand the ins and outs of securing speaking opportunities at high-profile conferences. I have personally worked with them in the past and have seen how they've supported clients' missions to further their thought-leadership objectives."

—Paul Wood,
Executive Vice President, Ketchum New York

"Speaking at conferences has been a key tool in building my CV and helping me grow my professional network. Getting the speaker proposal right is vital for landing a spot on a conference agenda. If speaking at a conference is your goal, Aurora and David's expertise will help you get there."

—Dr. Dwayne Cantrell,
Associate Vice President, Student Access and Support Services,
California State University, Northridge

"Developing a strong speaker's bureau can be one of the most important components of a public relations program for my clients. With potential customers in the audience, my clients get tremendous value from speaking at industry conferences. Making sure their speaker proposals give them a platform to tell their story is always the goal. Aurora and David know how to create a proposal that does exactly that."

—Kris Kraves,
Principal, Kraves PR

"As a member of the review committee for the national conference of my professional association, I've seen the good, the bad, and the ugly when it comes to speaker proposals. The best are always the ones that combine creativity with meaningful content and clearly show that the speaker will impart important knowledge to our audience. Aurora and David have written some of the best proposals we see every year. You will learn a great deal from their experience."

—John E. Paris,
Assistant Treasurer,
Rogers Corporation and Conference Task Force Member,
The Association for Financial Professionals

"When I launched my career as a certified health coach, I wanted public speaking to be a key part of growing my business. Aurora helped me create a speaker proposal that truly captured my passion for health education, and I'm pleased to say I've used it to secure a paid speaking opportunity with a public library system. It was great to submit a proposal I felt confident about and then to have it be accepted."

- Andrea Arellano,
Certified Health Coach

"*Get Picked*? I thought the book was about noses . . ."

—Rainn Wilson,
Actor & Author

GET PICKED

TIPS, TRICKS, AND TOOLS
FOR CREATING AN
IRRESISTIBLE
SPEAKER PROPOSAL

Aurora Gregory and David Pitlik

Get Picked: Tips, Tricks, and Tools for Creating an Irresistible Speaker Proposal
© 2016 Aurora Gregory and David Pitlik

First Edition, May 2016
Los Angeles, California

ISBN: 978-0-9975244-1-3

Editing: Shayla Eaton, CuriouserEditing.com
Cover Layout and Design: Lena Elizer, LenaElizer.com
Book Layout and Design: James Woosley, FreeAgentPress.com

Dedicated to Omar,

who never let us forget
that not all speaker proposals
are irresistible.

CONTENTS

Introduction: Start by Choosing Yourself

Lessons Learned from the Trenches 19

You Talkin' to Me? 20

This Book Is a Game-Changer 21

Chapter 1: What's in It for Me?

Why Should I Want to Speak, Anyway? 24

You Can't Afford Not to Speak 25

Fresh Fodder for That Résumé 26

Jewels for Your Performance Review 26

LinkedIn Loves Updates 27

Give 'Em Something to Talk About 27

You Know Stuff Other People Need to Know 28

Need New Clients? They're at Your Next Speaking Opportunity 28

Speak to Impact Others: The Rewards Will Come 30

Chapter 2: Finding Conferences and Events to Speak At

Where's My Audience? I'm Ready for My Close-Up! 34

Who Ya Talkin' To? 34

Figuring Out Who 35

Don't Despise the Day of Small Beginnings 39

Small Steps to a Bigger Stage..40

Let Your Reputation Precede You..40

Step Up and Say Hello...42

Work Your Network..43

Your Best Is Always in Demand 43

Chapter 3: Getting Started with Your Speaker Proposal

Going from Wishful Thinking to On the Program...48

Ignore the Rules at Your Peril 49

Beefing Up Your Presentation Team...50

Avoid Eeny, Meeny, Miny, Moe: How to Pick a Great Topic for Your Session 52

Up Your Odds by Tapping into What's Hot...53

Chapter 4: Creating a Speaker Proposal That Gets Picked

Writing Your Session Abstract: Thou Shall Not Be Boring..58

What's in a Name? Create a Session Title That Intrigues 59

Unleash Your Inner Storyteller: How to Create Drama 62

Three Simple Steps to Constructing Your Session Story 64

Brevity Is a Virtue: If Abe Could Do It, So Can You...70

One Size Does Not Fit All: Choosing the Right Type of Session 71

It Takes Two (or More) to Tango: How to Incorporate a Co-Presenter 73

Sweat the Small Stuff: Take Every Opportunity to Bolster Your Submission.................75

Chapter 5: Crafting a Great Presentation

Congratulations! You've Been Picked to Speak: Now What?..80

Create an Outline: The Roadmap for Your Presentation 81

Think Story: Engage Your Audience 83

What's Your Story? Four Steps for Turning Your Presentation into a Narrative............84

Hot Starts, Grabbers, and Transitions—Oh My!..88

Avoiding Death by PowerPoint 90

Appeal to the Eye: Visual Style Counts...91

Every Picture Tells A Story, Don't It? 92

Wrapping Up Your Presentation and Other Assorted Suggestions 93

Chapter 6: Resources and Helpful Hints

Other Stuff We Know You'll Need..98

After Giving Your Presentation, What's Next?..98

A Few Brief Words on How to Write a Short Bio...101

Questions to Ask Yourself When Preparing Your Session Description........................104

Dos and Don'ts 107

A Tasty Sampler of Speaker Submissions 110

Building a Speaker's Package 115

Putting Words in Your Mouth: Strong Versus Weak...117

Now You Know What We Know..120

About the Authors
About the Authors 121

Acknowledgments
Acknowledgments 125

Sources
Sources.. 129

FOREWORD

It's not whether you win or lose. Trying is all that really matters. Oh, who are we kidding? Don't we all love to win?

Honestly, we live in a world that values and rewards those who succeed. That's why being selected to speak at a conference matters. Getting picked means you're a winner. And that's not a bad thing, really.

I've been to my fair share of conferences and I've had the privilege of speaking at a number of them. And one thing I've learned is that we all have expertise worth sharing. You and the subject matter experts and key executives in your business have something important to say. These ideas would benefit your industry, raise your organization's profile, attract new clients, and help retain existing ones.

Getting picked as a speaker would grant a mantle of expertise that could help launch a startup or further amplify the brand of an enterprise that is already successful and well established.

And once a speaker gets picked for a single engagement, getting picked to speak at future events becomes just a little bit easier.

The thing is… how to get picked? Unfortunately, cutting in line won't work for this.

This book is all about getting picked. Aurora Gregory and David Pitlik, longtime friends and professional colleagues, have leveraged their extensive experience in public relations, marketing communications, and storytelling to develop proposals that have secured speaking slots for their clients at local, regional, national, and international conferences and packaged it up for us to put into practice.

When I was the Chief Marketing Officer of J. P. Morgan's Treasury Services business, I thought of Aurora and David as "my secret agents" in helping us get placements at the conferences where we thought the firm could add the greatest value for our clients, with the topics that our clients told us were important to them. The field was a crowded one, and competition for key slots was fierce. Yet, by working with Aurora and David, we managed to secure coveted slots for our subject matter experts time and time again. In my opinion, their expertise was a game-changer for us.

Crafting a proposal that secures a speaking slot is both art and science. It's not just being able to demonstrate proficiency in the subject matter, or convince the conference committee that the proposed speaker has the necessary oratory skills that can mesmerize an audience. It's knowing your personal strengths and opportunities, understanding the needs of the committee that is making the speaker selections, researching the topic and the organization so that you understand the competitive landscape, and then carefully constructing your proposal to fit that very special niche that no one else can fill. The tools you need to do this are right here in this book. Now you too have a secret agent, but I draw the line at divulging our super-secret handshake. Some things I just won't share.

In my opinion, Aurora and David are doing a tremendous public service by writing this book. I believe that readers who put the advice in this book into action will gain sought-after speaking slots, receive public recognition for their thought leadership, and the world will be so much smarter as a result of this knowledge-sharing! I know I will sleep better tonight secure in the knowledge that you are in good hands. Of course, that could just be because I was up way too early and I'm exhausted.

Eileen Zicchino
Former Chief Marketing Officer, J. P. Morgan Treasury Services

INTRODUCTION:
START BY CHOOSING YOURSELF

"You only live once, but if you do it right, once is enough."

—Mae West

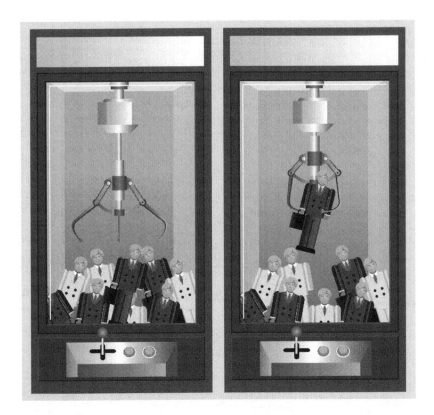

Remember that feeling on the grade school playground when all the kids gathered to play a game? Each captain alternately picked players from the crowd. The knot in your stomach kept growing tighter and tighter with every passing turn. And each time your name wasn't called, you were filled with an overwhelming feeling of dread and despair. Are your palms sweating just thinking about it?

Funny how some things in life never change. Submitting yourself to speak at an important industry conference is just like being back on that dusty playground. No matter how successful you've become in your professional life, once again someone else is deciding your fate and that just plain ol' stinks. No doubt you've got incredibly relevant ideas and indispensable wisdom to share with your peers and colleagues, but if you don't get picked to speak, no one will ever hear your brilliant thoughts. And to think you were convinced those sweaty-palm days were completely behind you!

Short of sponsoring your own conference, you will always be beholden to a selection committee who will decide your fate. But that doesn't mean there's nothing you can do to dramatically improve your odds of getting chosen. Simply having a compelling speaking topic may not be enough on its own. In fact, creating a winning speaker submission requires just as much savvy and skill as any important business proposal. That means putting in the time and effort to achieve the desired payoff—being invited to speak at the conference.

It's time to put the playground behind you and choose yourself. It's time to create speaker submissions that are so bold, so powerful, and so convincing that no committee will be able to say no.

It's time to be a winner.

Lessons Learned from the Trenches

Whether you are preparing a speaker submission for yourself, or for someone else, some basic rules of the road can help you achieve your goals. While many of these rules may seem straightforward, it is surprising how often submitters completely ignore them. That's why we decided to write this book. We wanted to pass along our collective wisdom from having written scores of successful speaker submissions for conferences around the world.

Over the years, we have helped organizations large and small break through the conference submission clutter by highlighting their great stories. It hasn't always been easy. Like anyone else, we've learned some hard lessons along the way. We've made mistakes. And we've had heartbreaking rejections. But over time, we've come to understand the intricacies of the submission process and how to maximize the chances of success.

Our primary goal with this book is to share what we've learned in the trenches so you can avoid the pitfalls. Our ultimate mission is to turn you into a speaker submission juggernaut. If your colleagues end up resenting your speaking success, just don't hold it against us!

You Talkin' to Me?

First things first: who should be reading this book?

✓ Professionals looking to become industry thought leaders

✓ Industry experts looking to raise their profile among their peer group

✓ Subject matter experts with a distinct success story, unique process, or distinct point of view

We *are* talking to you! Speaking at events, conferences, and trade shows is a great way to raise your profile in your industry and among your peers. You can use your speaking opportunities to build your résumé, strengthen your LinkedIn profile, and add to your list of accomplishments on your annual performance review. Don't sell yourself short—you have more experience, knowledge, and know-how than you realize.

If you've never spoken at a conference before and you're ready to establish yourself as a thought leader, *Get Picked* will help you plumb the knowledge you have so you can offer it in a compelling way.

You may be a seasoned thought leader who has spoken at some events, but maybe you want to increase your chances of being selected as a conference speaker in the future. You will learn how to take what you know and package it in a way that clearly lets conference organizers know you have powerful knowledge to share with their audience.

Regardless of your industry or area of expertise, if you have a success story to share, if you've developed a unique process that will make people's jobs easier, or if you have a distinct point of view on a particular topic, we can help you. We'll teach you how to frame your thoughts, views, and experiences so they attract the attention they deserve from the conferences that can move your business, your career, or your message to the next level.

This Book Is a Game-Changer

How to get selected to speak at conferences can seem like a mystery. If you've submitted a speaker proposal before, feeling confident that it was a slam dunk for making the agenda, you were probably disappointed and a little confused when you received the dreaded rejection email. While there's no way to guarantee a winning proposal for any conference, there are some things you can do to help your topic and expertise shine a little brighter and stand out from the crowd.

We want to help you deliver a stand-out proposal that's a perfect fit for the conference that's a perfect fit for you. And we want teach you the strategies and tactics that will simplify your process and focus your efforts such as:

- How to find conferences to pitch your expertise
- How to make your idea a hot topic
- What makes a great presentation title
- How to use storytelling to sell your presentation idea
- Making the most of the limited word counts most call-for-speakers allow
- Ensuring your presentation deck works for you and not against you

And a few other tools, tips, and tricks to help you stand out from the competition.

We're all about setting you up for success. That's what you'll find here—the tricks of the trade that we've developed over fifteen years of preparing speaker proposals and helping speakers get ready to deliver a conference session that is interesting, memorable, and well-evaluated.

On the following pages, we will help you understand why speaking at conferences is important, which venues make the most sense for you, how to create a winning submission, and how to prepare your presentation once you've been selected.

So let's get started!

CHAPTER 1:

WHAT'S IN IT FOR ME?

"Public speaking is leadership and organizations promote people with leadership qualities."
—Sarah Lloyd-Hughes

Why Should I Want to Speak, Anyway?

When our clients first began coming to us for help with se-curing speaking spots for their subject matter experts (that's you whether you know it or not at this point—you're a subject mat-ter expert!), the speaker proposals we created almost exclusively focused on what they could do to move the company's message forward. As we researched conferences to approach and worked on putting proposals together, we spent most of our time strategizing how the topics we were going to offer would help our client sell their product, their expertise, and their perspective.

There are some good reasons to make sharing what you know the primary focus of a speaker proposal, but making this the exclu-sive focus of a speaker placement campaign created limitations we struggled to overcome. We were able to secure some speaking slots but not nearly the number our clients wanted. We were stymied on how to turn the tide until we identified some key changes we need-ed to make to be more successful.

One of the things we failed to do was focus on how securing a speaker placement impacted the one person who is critical to the whole program: the actual speaker. It's important not to lose sight of the fact that the speaker also has much to gain from presenting at a conference, whether it be for reputation or the development of potential business prospects. In the end, a great presentation should be a win-win for the audience and the presenter.

You Can't Afford Not to Speak

Of all the people involved in the speaker placement process, the person who stands to benefit the most is you. In today's fast-moving and competitive environments, you need every advantage to help you stand out from the crowd of great professionals you're surrounded by every day in your workplace and in your industry. Frankly, you can't afford not to speak. Your career path, your business, your goals, your dreams, and your vision will benefit when you are seen as a dynamic, authoritative voice. And that requires sharing the wealth of knowledge you possess with audiences that need and want to hear what you know.

The number-one reason you need to become a conference speaker is because it immediately identifies you as a leader in your space. It does not matter what your topic or expertise is; if you are selected to speak at an industry conference that matters to your colleagues and peers—whether it's a corporate conference teeming with professionals eager to expand their knowledge and horizons, a craft or hobbyist event that gathers like-minded people to share the latest trends or developments, or a ministry conference that brings together people engaged in spreading the message of faith, hope, and love—you will immediately hold a leadership position that others can and will want to learn from and follow.

Regardless of whether you're speaking on your professional vocation or your personal passions, speaking makes you a leader and leaders get picked for opportunities that others don't.

Want to move your career, hobby, or ministry forward? Become a conference speaker.

Fresh Fodder for That Résumé

Updating your résumé is tough when your job hasn't changed or you haven't had an award or some other type of recognition bestowed upon you. But becoming a speaker gives you some fresh information to fluff up your résumé in a meaningful way. You may not be looking for a job or even considering a job search, but being able to add content to your résumé that highlights your expertise is always a plus. If you're a hobbyist or ministry leader, you can use your latest speaking gig to build up your speaker bio. Being a conference speaker positions you as an educator of your peers—and that's always a good thing.

Jewels for Your Performance Review

Another benefit of speaking is that you have new and interesting activities to include in your annual performance review. Speaking at conferences may even be part of your job description or your annual goals. Whether speaking is or isn't a goal you need to reach as an employee, being able to list "Speaker at XYZ Conference" on your job performance documents should land you extra consideration when it comes to compensation or promotion. You get extra points if it's not something you were asked to do—most employers see public speaking on behalf of the company as a big upside for the business, as well as the employee. You'll get positive marks for positioning your company, along with yourself, as a leader.

LinkedIn Loves Updates

Hannah Morgan reports in the Undercover Recruiter that job-seekers who updated their LinkedIn status weekly were ten times more likely to be contacted by recruiters.[1] Unless you've changed jobs or received a promotion or an award lately, having some career-relevant information to use as updated content can be challenging. But becoming a conference speaker gives you a status and profile update that you can share with your connections. Every time you get picked to speak, your first online stop should be LinkedIn for an update.

Give 'Em Something to Talk About

Everyone loves to brag about the cool people they know and the cool things they're doing. Getting selected as a conference speaker gives your company, your colleagues, your boss, your friends, your ministry partners, even your mom something to share about you. They can all tell others about your latest speaking gig. Word-of-mouth sharing by someone other than yourself extends your reputation as an expert and gives you third-party validation that can't be measured.

Bottom line: it's an honor and a feather in your cap to be chosen to be a conference speaker, and it can only enhance your career goals and vision. So speak up—your career will thank you later!

You Know Stuff Other People Need to Know

There's probably nothing more rewarding than helping someone solve a problem, figure out an easier way to do something, or learn something new. Through your experiences, your successes, and your failures, you know things that others don't, which could improve their work (or personal) lives, set them up for success, and enable them to achieve the milestones you have.

Need New Clients?
They're at Your Next Speaking Opportunity

Jennifer was in the process of transitioning her consulting business. She was moving away from working with corporations and helping them grow their brand recognition to using her years of brand-building experience to help executives develop their personal brands and grow their careers. She had developed an entire suite of tools for this new target audience but was having trouble getting new clients to sign on.

Her solution? She booked speaking engagements with professional groups in her area to talk about the importance of individual professional brand-building. These small group presentations gave her the platform she needed to educate potential clients on why investing in their professional brand was critical and allowed her to showcase her expertise and her ability and availability to help them.She's had amazing results, building her list of prospects and signing several new clients following each presentation. Her clientele is growing and now, professional groups are seeking her out as a speaker for their meetings.

Finding new prospects is not always easy. Cold-calling and emailing can be ineffective and sometimes the word-of-mouth pipeline can dry up. Conference speaking puts you in front of a group of prospects and allows you to show them what you can do for them—solve their most challenging problems, give them the extra bandwidth they're looking for, or give them a taste of the perspective you can bring to their business.

So, if you're a consultant to any professional segment—business, education, healthcare, ministry, or whatever your area of focus—adding speaking at conferences or professional associations (national, regional, and local) to your marketing mix can be just the tool you need to reach new clients and grow your business.

Speak to Impact Others: The Rewards Will Come

It's a powerful thing to impact someone else's business practices, career, or life trajectory. By sharing what you know, you're in a position to do just that. So don't keep the good stuff to yourself. Get out there and share what you know with people who need to know it. You'll get more than you've given, while opening up the possibility of making an impact beyond your own immediate world.

And by sharing the knowledge you have, you'll be rewarded with new connections, new career opportunities, and new clients. Your résumé and career will grow and you'll find you suddenly have avenues you never imagined open to you.

The Big Takeaways:

☐ **Step into the Spotlight:** Becoming a conference speaker immediately identifies you as a leader in your space.

☐ **Claim Your Bragging Rights:** Speaking at conferences gives you fresh content to add to your bio, résumé, and LinkedIn profile. Conference presentations are great to mention during your annual performance evaluation.

☐ **Reel In Some Big New Fish:** Conference presentations are a great way to engage with new or existing client prospects. Your presentation showcases what you know and how it can help them.

☐ **Build It and They Will Come:** Impacting your audience in a meaningful way should be your key goal. The rewards and benefits you seek will follow.

CHAPTER 2:

FINDING CONFERENCES AND EVENTS TO SPEAK AT

"The success of your presentation will be judged not by the knowledge you send but by what the listener receives."

—Lilly Walters

Where's My Audience? I'm Ready for My Close-Up!

Now that you're convinced getting out there and sharing your expertise publicly with your peers, colleagues, and your professional universe can only help you reach your goals, you've got to find the right audience. It's a safe bet that no matter the topic, there's a group with a common interest, professional pursuit, or singular focus that gathers in one form or fashion to learn from one another and network together. You just need to find the group that fits your interests, and then find out when they meet and how they select speakers.

Finding your audience is about defining *who* they are and *where* they gather.

Who Ya Talkin' To?

Finding the group (or groups) that want to learn from you can be easy and hard at the same time.

A technology company we're acquainted with was extremely anxious to speak in front of industry groups and related audiences. Looking to build a list of potential conferences, they researched literally hundreds of events to find the right ones to pitch their executives and topics for speaking slots.

It was a daunting task that was overwhelming, exhausting, frustrating, and ultimately, unfruitful. They spent a lot of time looking at conferences that were not a fit for them at all and because they were essentially looking for love in all the wrong places, they missed opportunities to offer speaker proposals for events that would have been a perfect fit for them.

The key to finding an audience for your expertise is knowing specifically who they are and where they go to learn to be better at what they do. This is true whether you're an accountant, a teacher, an event planner, or a ministry leader. When you know where the cool kids hang out, you can create your plan to hang with them as a speaker.

Figuring Out Who

Defining your audience clearly is the single most important thing you can do to raise your chances of being picked as a conference speaker. When conference organizers evaluate the many (and sometimes many, many) speaker proposals,  they need to know you understand who their attendees are and what they want or need to hear. Knowing who they are and what they want to learn will help you sharpen your speaker proposal so it is irresistible to conference organizers. Not defining your audience almost guarantees your proposal will be a weak fit at best or will face certain rejection at worst.

Use these guidelines for defining your perfect audience:

- Your audience is going to be people within the same profession as you, regardless of industry, with the same title, the title above yours, or the title below yours. Some examples:
  - Finance and banking professionals (treasurers, CFOs, bankers)
  - Communications executives (corporate communications, internal communications, public relations)
  - Human resource professionals (executive recruiters, organizational development)
  - IT professionals (programmers, web developers, corporate IT pros)
  - Healthcare professionals (nurses, doctors, administrators)
  - Law enforcement (sworn officers, civilian officers)
  - Educators (teachers, school administrators)
  - Ministry leaders/lay workers (pastors, Sunday school teachers, worship leaders)
- Consider audience categories that cut across professions:
  - If you're a finance professional for a healthcare system, include finance professionals and healthcare finance professionals.
  - You might be a school nurse. You'll want to have traditional nursing professionals as well as school nurses on your list.
  - Are you a technology professional? Consider adding other professionals that make deep use of technology— banking, telecommunications, and entertainment could all potentially have an interest in what you can share.

Let's break down an example. Say you are a human resources executive and part of the organizational development team for your company. Your list of audiences might look something like this:

- General human resource professionals
- Organizational development professionals
- Training professionals
- Executives leading teams

Now that you've got a list of audience members, you can figure out where they go to meet, learn, and network. Your Internet search is going to include searches like these:

- HR Conferences
- HR Leadership Conferences
- Executive Talent Conferences

Your search will lead you to results like these:

- The Human Capital Summit
- SHRM
- Employee Engagement Conference
- HR West
- HR in Hospitality
- Association for Financial Professionals
- Talent Management Conference

Now that you have this list, you can visit each site and check for their conference dates and the process for submitting a speaker proposal (more on that later). You'll execute this process for each target audience you are trying to reach.

Another tool you can use to search for conference events is a conference search engine. These are aggregators of conference events that act as directories for meeting and event planners. They are usually put together by conference production companies that use them to draw event planners to their site and encourage them to use their services to produce conference events. Anyone can use these conference search engines, including you!

These are great tools if you have an area of interest that you're searching but are not getting much from your Internet search. Keep in mind that the search engine is only as good as the listings it holds. Conference and event planners are invited to post their events in the search engine. If they don't post their event, you won't find it there. Some search engines focus on a particular industry or topic area, which is great since the focus of the events you are searching is already narrowed for you.

Some search engines you can use:

General Conference Search Engines:

- AllConferences.com
- ListOfConference.org
- Lanyrd.com
- EventsinAmerica.com
- 10Times.com

Industry or Topic-Specific Search Engines:

- ConfSearch.com — focuses on computer science conferences
- ConferenceAlerts.com — focuses on academic conferences globally
- SearchEngineLand.com — focuses on events for SEO marketing professionals

Don't Despise the Day of Small Beginnings

Getting picked to speak at large, national, or even international conference events is a great way to build exposure for you and your expertise. But you don't have to wait for a big conference that interests you to pitch your session. Most professional associations and interest-based organizations have local and state chapters that hold monthly or annual conferences of their own. They need to present an agenda to their attendees just like the national or international events do, and they would be very interested in learning about what you have to share. Don't overlook the value and benefits that investing in speaking at smaller events can bring. Small events can deliver big returns to your career, your business, and your message.

There are benefits and advantages to speaking at local, state, or regional events:

- There are more opportunities—local chapters have monthly meetings so they need twelve times as many speakers per year, giving you twelve chances to speak instead of the one offered at a national event.

- There is often less competition for speaking spots at local events and preference is usually given to local experts. Make geography work for you by scoping out events that are closer to your home base.

- There is less out-of-pocket expense for you since you likely won't have to travel as far to get to the event—you might even be able to do it after work or at midday if you are selected to speak at a lunch event. National conferences don't normally pay for your travel expenses so this could be a huge cost savings.

Small Steps to a Bigger Stage

Speaking at local events also gives you a chance to develop your speaking skills with smaller audiences that can be less intimidating than the larger audiences you'll find at national conferences.

Local events will give you the chance to present your material to a live audience and get their feedback. You can refine your presentation based on your local audience's reaction, giving you the chance to add in or take out content in response to their questions or responses. This will help you fine-tune your session and get it ready to offer to a larger event. Think of this like an off-Broadway preview before you step into the bright lights of the big leagues.

Let Your Reputation Precede You

You can use speaking at local events to make important contacts with local chapter leadership that could prove helpful to you at the national levels of an organization. Present a great session at a state conference, and you can ask state leadership to recommend you for consideration to the national conference when they are asked for speaker suggestions.

We once worked with an assistant treasurer who was invited to be a presenter at a regional chapter of the professional association where she was a member. The regional conference draws a much smaller audience than the national event. She did such a great job that when the time came to select speakers for the national conference, she submitted her topic and was immediately picked to present. The time she invested in presenting at the regional event paid off when it was time for selections to be made for a larger stage.

Don't forget about speaking to community groups in your area. Your topic might be an ideal fit for your local chamber of commerce or other business networking group, Rotary, or Kiwanis chapter, or other service clubs. Check into the college and career group at your local college or university; offer to do your presentation for them. These organizations are often hungry for great content from great presenters. You have what they need, so don't be shy about offering it to them. Remember, the goal is to build your experience as a speaker and the best way to do that is to get in front of an audience.

Other groups that could be just the platform you're looking for include:

- Business networking groups — Business Networking International and Local Business Network are two you might consider.

- Special interest clubs — Photography, mothers of preschoolers, crafters, movies, home cooks, and more have local groups. Check into Meetup.com or other social meetup websites to find clubs and organizations and their point of contact or start with a Google search.

- Local business publications — City business journals and city magazines all host events that need speakers for their programs.

- Your clients — Offer to do a "lunch and learn" meeting for your client's staff. You'll get a presentation opportunity and build goodwill with your client.

And finally, don't neglect checking out where your peers are speaking. Their speaking opportunities will give you ideas for other outlets you can explore.

Step Up and Say Hello

Getting picked to speak at a local, state, or regional event can be a little different than getting picked for a national event.

At the local level, your best bet is going to be to reach out directly to the organization and offer to speak at an upcoming meeting. Find the group's website and look for the name of the person who  is responsible for booking speakers—they usually hold the title of *events chairperson* or *education chairperson*. If you don't find anyone holding that title, look for the president of the group. And absent that, you'll look for their information form.

From there, you'll want to prepare an email introducing yourself and the topic you want to share with the group. The email needs to include all the details you would include if you were submitting your proposal to a national event using their process. Include the title of your presentation, the session summary, and very clear specifics on what the group will take away from your presentation. Be sure to include your bio and contact information beyond your email address so they can call you to discuss your participation.

Remember, local organizations are often staffed by volunteers who are elected to their roles by the membership. Give them some time to get back to you, but don't be shy about following up. Don't pester them, but do let them know that you're very interested in sharing with their group. If they call you, get back to them promptly to lock in a date.

Work Your Network

Whether we realize it or not, we all have a network and we are all part of someone else's network. In the past, networking was about meeting great people and brokering an introduction to someone you really wanted to meet through a mutual connection. That's still what it is today, but now we also have the digital world to make connections. The opportunity to establish, cultivate, and benefit from your network has never been riper.

Your network can help you research conferences and meetings that would be perfect for you to pitch your topic and offer yourself as a speaker. Ask your peers, colleagues, and fellow enthusiasts what events they attend and then research the event to find a speaker contact or define the speaker submission process. The people you connect with can help you find the audience(s) that want and need to hear your knowledge.

On the digital side, use your LinkedIn contacts and your membership in LinkedIn groups to help you source speaking opportunities. Monitor what events your network is attending. Be active in your groups, offering your expertise to people searching for speakers. Respond to calls for speakers posted by others in the groups you're a part of or give them leads on colleagues that would be a perfect fit for the spot they are trying to fill.

You're an expert in your field, on your topic, and on your passion. And great people know great people. Let all the great people you know and interact with help you source the speaking opportunities you're looking for.

Your Best Is Always in Demand

Always give every audience your very best. Large or small, national or local, you want those who give you their attention to walk away with the best presentation you can give them. Don't let size dictate how much time you put into preparing and rehearsing your material. Every audience deserves your best.

Speaking to an audience, large or small, will yield so many benefits that can only help boost your career, your goals, and your dreams. You'll make new connections that could lead to business referrals or job opportunities. But it all starts with finding the right venues that will get you in front of the audience or audiences that need to hear your message.

The Big Takeaways:

☐ **Getting to Know You:** Knowing who your audience is and where they gather is the key to finding the best places to present.

☐ **Think Outside the Proverbial Box:** Don't limit your target audiences to just your peers. Consider cross-functional audiences to expand your reach.

☐ **Do Your Homework First:** Conference organizers need to know that you understand who attends their events and what they want to know or learn.

☐ **Search and You Shall Find:** Conference search engines will help you generate a list of conferences to approach with a speaker proposal.

☐ **Start Small to Go Big:** Local, state, and regional events can be great stepping-stones and can help you build your reputation as a speaker, allowing you to land speaking spots at larger events.

☐ **You Can Try with a Little Help from Your Friends:** Your professional network can be a great source for landing a speaking gig. Let it be known among your peers that you're interested in sharing on a particular topic.

CHAPTER 3:

GETTING STARTED WITH
YOUR SPEAKER PROPOSAL

*"The only impossible journey is
the one you never begin."*
—Anthony Robbins

"Today we are going to find out if you can make that leap."

Going from Wishful Thinking to On the Program

Once you've done your homework and identified the ideal conference to speak at, the real fun begins. You'll need to razzle-dazzle the selection committee, demonstrating that your expertise and your chosen topic are not only worthy of the inclusion at the conference, but will be a surefire draw for attendees.

The speaker submission itself is really nothing more than a brief synopsis of your talk, but it must be expertly crafted in order to stand out. Think of it like your college application. Sure, terrific grades made you academically worthy, but let's face it: lots of kids had similarly outstanding grade point averages. That's why it was so important to highlight your extracurricular activities. They helped the admissions board see beyond the grades to understand what made you special and truly worthy of acceptance to their institution.

Luckily, getting selected at a conference doesn't require a high SAT score. But standing out is still the goal. Your speaker submission has to do more than just lay out the bare facts of your presentation.

It has to tell a story and present you as a dynamic speaker who will command attention.

Ignore the Rules at Your Peril

A common mistake many submitters make is to completely ignore the submission rules and guidelines. This is akin to assembling a bed frame from Ikea without following the directions.  You'll probably end up with a wobbly, three-legged frame, which means you'll most likely be sleeping on the floor.

Each conference has its own criteria and rules for its speaker submissions. It's important to start your submission process by studying and understanding these guidelines. They may include:

- The word limit for each section of the submission.
- The number of speakers allowed to participate in a single presentation.
- Acceptable session format, such as a lecture, workshop, roundtable, debate, case study, or industry panel.
- Acceptable participants, such as industry practitioners (these would be your peers), analysts, educators, third-party vendors, industry association representatives, and consultants.
- Strict adherence to peer-to-peer educational content that doesn't sell or market.
- Session length.
- Previous experience as a presenter.

Believe it or not, the selection committee *will* give you points for following the rules. It won't cement your inclusion on the conference program, but it may make the difference between being strongly considered or dismissed out of hand.

Beefing Up Your Presentation Team

Depending on the individual conference requirements, you may find it advantageous to include additional presenters as part of your team. Being able to offer a range of perspectives and insights can be highly attractive to the selection committee. After all, they're looking for presentations that will have the broadest appeal and the most impactful educational content.

Another factor to consider is the marquee value of your presenting team. Big-name companies, well-known experts, and respected influencers tend to attract a good audience at conferences. Everyone wants to know how industry leaders achieve their success. So, selection committees tend to favor big-name presenters. If you're a smaller player, you might consider teaming up with a marquee presenter to increase your odds of selection.

In addition to big names, selection committees are also swayed by any presenters who might offer a unique perspective. For instance, if you're an HR professional talking about developing high-achieving staffers, including a current or retired NFL coach to discuss leadership development would add tremendous appeal and, dare we say, buzzworthy-ness to your presentation. Industry analysts, educators, and consultants can also make a good addition to your team, because they tend to bring an unbiased, third-party perspective to the discussion.

Now don't let all this talk about big names deter you if you're just a "little guy." A great presentation topic with a solid presenter can still make the grade, even without a heavy weight on the roster. It just means your submission has to be all that much stronger to ensure you stand out.

Most conferences focus primarily on practitioners. This doesn't mean that vendors can't submit, but they do need to include a practitioner as part of their team. Ignoring this one rule of thumb can spell doom for  your submission. Including a practitioner is actually a great idea anyway, because it allows you to bring credibility and provide the perspective of someone who has firsthand experience with your solution or service. And it's a great way to keep your presentation from being an overt sales pitch, which would probably get you rejected.

PRO TIP:
DON'T BE AFRAID TO INVITE THE HOST.

A clever way to improve your odds with the selection committee is by inviting a representative from the conference themselves to be a co-presenter. Of course, this trick only works in very specific instances where the topic warrants.

Avoid Eeny, Meeny, Miny, Moe:
How to Pick a Great Topic for Your Session

Once you've identified the conference you want to speak at, you will now have to decide the topic of your session. The *eeny, meeny, miny, moe* selection technique is not recommended. Of course, if you already have a clear idea for your session, all you need to do is make sure it fits one of the topic area buckets. Most conferences list the topic areas on their website, outlining what sessions will fit the parameters of each topic. These lists are often called

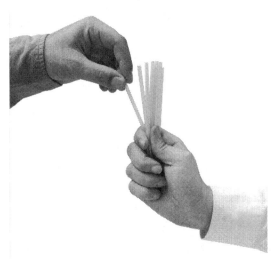

tracks and help conference organizers compose an agenda that is balanced around key areas of focus. You may find that your session is a good fit in more than one topic area. Some conferences may allow you to submit the same session in more than one area, while others may make you choose.

More often than not, if the selection committee really likes your session idea, they will move you to what they deem the most appropriate topic area. If you are proposing more than one session, consider placing them in different topic areas to increase your odds of getting one selected. If you put them all in the same topic area, you run the risk of competing against yourself. Keep in mind, there are usually a limited number of speaking slots in each topic area, so the more buckets you can place yourself in, the better your odds.

Up Your Odds by Tapping into What's Hot

A winning speaker submission has to have an appealing topic. Don't forget, the conference is looking for speakers who will offer the broadest range of attendees with sessions that grab their attention, luring them with must-see presentations.

When considering session topics, always keep conference attendees in mind; after all, that's exactly what the selection committee will be doing too! If you come up with a topic that attendees are sure to clamor for, there's a good chance your speaker submission will be selected.

If you are not sure what would make an appealing speaking topic, a good place to start brainstorming is the conference website. In many cases, the conference will provide a list of hot topics, outlining areas they believe will appeal to the attendees. These areas represent a good jumping-off point in developing your session topic.

So what makes a great session topic? The answer to that question might be right under your nose. Consider topics that are pressing issues with your staff or organization, such as things that keep you up at night and drive internal conversations. If you are wanting to present at a special interest, hobbyist, or even ministry conference, think about the topics, challenges, or ongoing conversations you have with others in your interest group. Chances are good, if you're focusing on it, others will be interested in it too.

You'll also want to consider topics that are important to your business. You may have a totally hot topic, but if it doesn't help to move your business, your profile, or your influence forward, it's not going to do you much good. Be sure to pick a topic that has a good balance of helping you and helping the conference audience.

Here are some questions you can ask yourself to uncover potential session topics:

- Do you have a fresh, compelling perspective on a common problem?
- Did you tackle a problem in a new, unique, or groundbreaking way?
- Are you using tools, technologies, or solutions that are reengineering or revolutionizing processes?
- Have you accomplished something that truly rises to the level of best practice?
- Are you dealing with industry or regulatory issues in a way that others would benefit from in their business dealings?
- Have you achieved a major success through ingenuity or reinvention?
- Have you come up with a new way to use standard or basic tools?
- Can you share how you or your team have developed a new way to address target audiences or the people you serve?
- Is there a product line that's delivering big results for clients that you can talk about?
- Is there a fresh take on a message or concept you want to move beyond your current sphere of influence?

The Big Takeaways:

☐ **Paint Inside the Lines:** Rules aren't always meant to be broken. Don't annoy the selection committee by blatantly ignoring their carefully conceived submission guidelines.

☐ **Bring Your A-Game and Your A-Team:** When putting together a team of presenters, think about who will offer the broadest perspective and who will draw in attendees.

☐ **Avoid the Round Hole if Your Presentation Is a Square Peg:** Carefully choose the right conference track for your presentation. If submitting more than one topic, be strategic and try to submit in different tracks so you don't compete against yourself.

☐ **Pick an Irresistible Topic:** The most appealing topics for selection committees are usually the ones that are the hottest subjects with conference attendees. Choose a topic that's buzzworthy and you'll dramatically up your odds of getting picked to speak!

☐ **Your Topic Should Be Hot, but Also Move the Needle:** If your topic doesn't align with the goals you have for your business in addition to being a fit for the conference, you miss out on a chance to move your business to the next level. Make sure your topic is a win-win for you and the conference.

CHAPTER 4:

CREATING A SPEAKER PROPOSAL THAT GETS PICKED

"Be yourself; everyone else is already taken."

—Oscar Wilde

Writing Your Session Abstract: Thou Shall Not Be Boring

We've all seen those iconic Dos Equis beer commercials about the "Most Interesting Man in the World."[2] It's hard not to chuckle as the sonorous voice of the announcer matter-of-factly describes the prowess of the bearded, debonair gentleman who "is the life of parties that he has never attended." Or "who once won a staring contest with his own reflection."

Fortunately, you don't have to be the most interesting man or woman in the world to create a fascinating session description that will turn more heads than a supermodel.

One of the guiding principles in writing a great session abstract is, "Thou shall not be boring." Keep in mind that your proposal should not only showcase the educational value of your topic, but should also communicate that it will be fun for attendees. If you can add drama and interest to your topic, while also showing your passion for the subject matter, you'll be off to an excellent start. Never lose sight of the fact that you have something important to share, and this abstract is your opportunity to make the case for why attendees will be interested.

So, now the time has come to write your session abstract. For some, writing is a nerve-wracking, nail-biting endeavor. For others, it's a welcomed creative challenge. Whichever group you fall into, there are some simple tricks of the trade to help ensure your session description is well written and, just as importantly, well received. Writing your session abstract need not be a torturous exercise if you keep the conference rules in mind, organize your thoughts first, and always remember your audience.

What's in a Name?
Create a Session Title That Intrigues

Whoever said "you should never judge a book by its cover" clearly wasn't talking about conference session titles. The first thing any selection committee will read is your submission title, which is why it's so important. This is your first chance to grab attention and make a splash. Simply put—don't squander it! Beyond catching the attention of the selection committee, your title will also need to entice attendees to add your session to their conference schedules if you're selected. After all, the bottom line for the committee is: what sessions will best fulfill our educational objectives and which topics will draw the biggest crowds?

More often than not, submission criteria will set a limit for the length of the title, either through a maximum number of words or characters. A short limit for the title certainly makes your job all the more challenging, but keep in mind, everyone submitting a session faces the same hurdle, so this is, in reality, an excellent opportunity to stand out.

PRO TIP:
DON'T IGNORE TITLE LENGTH RESTRICTIONS.

Nothing says, "I don't really care about your conference rules" or "obviously I haven't even bothered to read them" like a title that's outside the established limit. Trust us, this is not the best way to make a favorable impression on the selection committee. We know it's not as much fun having to color between the lines, but this is one of those times following the rules actually does make a difference.

Many approach the title as little more than a formality. Sort of like a brief appetizer before the main course. But nothing could be further from the truth. Your title is a crucial opportunity to show that you are a force to be reckoned with and your session description should not be ignored!

When it comes to developing a cracker-jack title, creativity is a big plus. A clever turn of phrase can amp up interest in your session. The objective behind your title should be to build drama while at the same time communicating what your presentation will cover. Yes, this can be a tall order, but if you nail it, you'll have a considerable leg up on the competition.

A good title describes what the session is about. A great title will tell potential attendees what they'll learn, while at the same time creating a bit of intrigue.

Here are a few examples of pedestrian titles and a corresponding creative one:

RUN-OF-THE-MILL SESSION TITLE:	CATCHY SESSION TITLE:
"How Businesses Are Combatting Fraud"	"Kicking Fraudsters to the Curb: Business Best Practices You Can't Live Without"
"Converting Paper Records into Electronic Files to Achieve Critical Operational Efficiency Gains"	"Give Yourself a Papercut: How Technology Can Completely Transform Your Operations"
"Educational Teaching Techniques for the Modern Classroom"	"How I Cured Nose-Picking with Duct Tape and Other Crazy Ideas That Improved Learning"
"Decorating on a Budget"	"Family First: Putting Your Priorities in Order in the Age of Digital Distraction"
"Tools for Evangelizing"	"Go Fish! Creative Ways to Draw People to Christ"
"Creating Leadership Buy-In: The First Step in Change Management"	"Don't Put the Cart Before the Horse: How to Secure Leadership Buy-In to Ensure Project Success"
"Discover the Leader Within"	"Unleash Your Inner-Leadership Beast"
"Learning to Go with the Flow"	"Embrace the Chaos: An Exercise in Making the Most of Randomness"
"What to Do with Half-Finished Projects"	"Breathing Life into Your UFOs (Un-Finished Objects)"

In addition to framing the topic of your presentation, a title can include key benefits the audience will learn about. Driving efficiency, introducing radical new innovations, reallocating precious resources, or reengineering outdated processes—these are all key buzzwords that will grab attention and set the stage for a fascinating talk.

A title can also include a significant milestone that was achieved. For example, if you're going to talk about how you saved your company a million dollars, you might want to include that in the title. Your peers will no doubt be interested in hearing how they can accomplish a similar feat.

When creating a winning session title, it's important to keep in mind that first and foremost, it should communicate the key takeaway of your session. Being clever just for clever's sake won't help you get selected if your title doesn't actually describe what the session will be about. It's important that a title be impactful, compelling, and concise. Wasted or extra words don't help, so cut them. And whenever possible, try to infuse the drama of your proposal into the title, tempting attendees to see that this is a can't-miss session.

Unleash Your Inner Storyteller: How to Create Drama

Everyone loves a good story. From a tender young age, we learn the allure of storytelling and how it can capture our imagination. While a session description may not rank up there with the tales of Harry Potter, it should still be a story. And the more interesting you can make that story, the better your chances of intriguing the selection committee and getting picked.

Before we discuss how to turn your session description into a compelling story, let's start by defining what a story is. It's safe to say we all know a story when we see or hear it, but defining what a story is can be a bit trickier. Here's a simple definition from Kendall Haven's *Story Proof: The Science Behind the Startling Touch of Story*. In his book, Haven considers a story to be "a narrative about a character overcoming some obstacle to achieve some important goal."[3]

It may sound almost too simple, but believe it or not, that is the basis for all well-constructed stories. Just as an example, let's take Herman Melville's classic novel, *Moby-Dick*. In this iconic story, the ship's crewman, Ishmael, gets caught up in Captain Ahab's obsession to seek revenge on the great white whale for destroying his ship and severing his leg on a previous voyage. After all members of the crew perish in an epic chase and then battle with Moby-Dick, only Ishmael survives to retell this cautionary tale. In *Moby-Dick*, Ishmael overcomes great odds on his way to fulfilling his dream to have an extraordinary whaling adventure.

You don't need to have a life-or-death struggle with an albino leviathan to inject drama into your session description. But the basic concept of overcoming a struggle and attaining a goal is the secret to creating a rich and intriguing story.

Three Simple Steps to Constructing Your Session Story

Ready to turn your session description into an engaging story? Let's get started. It's important to remember that while you may consider your topic pretty darn interesting, if your write-up doesn't convey all the elements that make it compelling, then you might be the only one who shares that view. Applying some basic storytelling principles can help you lay out the session description in a way that grabs attention, creates drama, and hopefully makes it irresistible to the committee or task force who will be making the conference speaker selections.

1) In the beginning:

Start by setting up the common challenges that you and your potential session attendees face. God may have created the earth in six days, but without the advantage of divine intervention, most corporate problems are highly complex and require overcoming significant hurdles. These may include common headaches you share, things that keep you up at night, obstacles that you and your organization faced—all of which drove you to seek solutions. Challenges can include everything from economic conditions, regulatory restrictions, process shortcomings, lack of technology, management hurdles, and so on. Be sure to keep your audience in mind when setting up the problem. The more they can relate to the situation you faced, the more likely they will want to hear how you addressed the problem. Applying Haven's definition of *story*, this is your opportunity to lay out the obstacle(s) you had to overcome to achieve your goal. This sets the dramatic stage for the solution that follows.

EXAMPLES OF SETTING UP STORY DRAMA:

★ As baby boomers are rapidly aging out of the workforce, human resource professionals are facing a tremendous brain drain in the senior ranks of their organizations, leading to increased pressure to cultivate the next generation of leaders.

★ With 25 percent of millennials putting off obtaining their driver's licenses, the automotive marketplace is facing a potentially catastrophic loss of its future consumer base, leaving critical questions for the future of the industry.[4]

★ As mandates for the Patient Protections and Affordable Care Act come into force, many employers remain uncertain about the implications to their businesses and are keeping a close watch on upcoming Supreme Court decisions that may undermine major parts of the health reform law.

---

2) Building the yellow brick road:

Now that you've briefly laid out the challenges, you'll want to paint a compelling picture of how you addressed these problems and implemented solutions that delivered noteworthy results. Stealing a little *Wizard of Oz* imagery, this is where you'll describe how you built your yellow brick road to a successful outcome. Once again, it's important to keep your fellow practitioners in mind as you lay out this part of your story. Think of it this way: if you could talk one-on-one to a peer who's facing the same issue, what would you tell him or her? The middle of your story continues to build the drama by outlining the steps you have taken to overcome all of your challenges.

Some examples of these steps might include:

- How you developed a new process.
- How you worked with different departments to achieve success.
- Or how you innovated a new way to use technology.

This is your opportunity to describe your best practices and explain why they were so important for your organization. Remember, don't try to include all the granular details of your approach; you'll cover that in your actual presentation. Here you just need to hit the high notes so you can whet the selection committee's and your audience's appetites. Get this right, and you'll be the wizard behind the curtain!

PRO TIP:
START BY FORMULATING THE BONES OF YOUR TOPIC.

If you're unsure how to formulate the heart of your description, we recommend that you start by bulleting out the top two or three messages that succinctly capture what your presentation is about. Once you've got those main points, you can simply add some meat to the bones and flesh out your story.

EXAMPLES OF HOW TO FRAME
THE HEART OF YOUR PRESENTATION:

★ The twenty-first-century classroom is all about engaging students using the tools they already know and use, which are primarily technology-based. In this presentation, we will explore the creative use of technology in the classroom and how to ensure quality teacher practice. We will discuss balancing accountability with innovation and how these tools can be used to stimulate effective learning.

★ Ensuring an enjoyable shopping experience is of paramount concern to retailers, which is why new innovations are being implemented to engage customers. In this session, our panel of industry experts will explore how cutting-edge technologies, such as smartphone apps, location beacons, Wi-Fi access points, wearable devices, and digital signs, are being used to deliver real contextual insights into customer preferences and behaviors to dramatically enhance the shopping experience.

★ No marketing tool today has the impact video has on audiences. In this session, attendees will learn about the latest trends in marketing with mobile video and hear from practitioners on how mobile web and apps can drive engagement, increase conversions, and build brands.

PRO TIP:
REMEMBER, IT'S NOT ALL ABOUT YOU.

While it may seem like semantics, shifting the language from "here's what we learned" to "here's what attendees will learn" can make a big difference in the eyes of the folks reviewing your submission. This simple trick can dramatically improve your odds of selection!

3) The big payoff:

Wrap up your session description with a brief explanation of what you achieved. This is the happy ending to your story—the part where you achieved your goal. It's okay to toot your horn a little bit. Everyone loves a success story.

Things you might include as your ending could be:

- A new process that saved your company millions of dollars.
- Your ability to cut the time it takes your staff to execute processes by half.
- How you managed to get a monster-sized project done in record time.
- The fact that you and your team have become an invaluable resource to your company and your leadership team.
- Your business has grown by double digits.
- You and your team were recognized by a company or industry award.

- Other people, departments, divisions, or companies are duplicating your process.

These kinds of success-related results validate the importance of your session and can be used to wrap up a stand-out description. That said, it's vitally important to frame everything in your session in terms of what attendees will take away. A common mistake is to focus solely on your own accomplishments. It's important to be crystal clear that attendees will come away with valuable insights that they can apply to their own organizations, classrooms, or workplace.

EXAMPLES OF HOW TO WRAP UP YOUR PROPOSAL:

★ We will share how technology improvements have led to significant efficiency gains in managing the supply chain, saving the organization $1 million a year, and dramatically improving the bottom line.

★ Attendees will learn how this government agency was able to implement process improvements that ultimately reduced costs by 60 percent, drove tremendous staff efficiency, and freed up vital resources to focus on the critical task of supporting constituents.

★ We will reveal how this simple design concept has turned the lighting industry on its ear and how game-changing innovation from a garage-based company has exploded into a $500-million-a-year business.

Brevity Is a Virtue:
If Abe Could Do It, So Can You

Most session descriptions have a fixed word limit. These limits are often a few hundred words. So, is it even possible to tell a complete story in so few words? Consider this: Abraham Lincoln's Gettysburg Address, one of the most famous speeches in American history, was a mere 278 words long. If good ol' Abe could tell a gripping story about our nation's struggle for liberty in only a few brief paragraphs, you can tell your story just as succinctly and hopefully as memorably.

Being economical in your word choices is a true art. Reread your session description with an eye toward cutting out any extraneous verbiage. The tighter your description, the more on point and clear your language is, the better the chances are that you'll drive home the important details and message of your session description. Be on the lookout for redundancy or overly complicated explanations. Simple, short sentences are your best friend. They are also more direct and easier to follow. And the fewer wasted words you have, the more space you'll have to focus on the specifics that will enable the selection committee to fully understand what you'll be sharing with attendees. Your goal is to be impactful, be compelling, and most importantly, be concise. Becoming president might not depend on it, but getting picked to speak at a conference certainly will.

When we work with clients, we interview them to learn more about the topic they want to propose. You can find a list of the questions we ask clients most often to draw out the most important details of the story they want to tell. You'll find a list of those questions on page 103 in Resources and Helpful Hints. Use them as a guide to help you frame up your topic and define your session description.

One Size Does Not Fit All: Choosing the Right Type of Session

Many conferences offer their speakers a choice of session types, allowing them to pick the one that best suits the nature of their presentation. These generally include:

- Case study/best practices
- Panel/roundtable discussions
- Industry updates
- Professional development

The type of session you plan to offer will impact how you write your session submission. The following are some basic guidelines:

★ Case Study: If you are planning to present a case study, you will want your session description to describe how best practices were developed and then employed to achieve a successful outcome. The story you tell in this format should start with the challenge, outline the solution, and conclude with the results, much like a traditional case study. For an example of a case study session description, see page 111 in Resources and Helpful Hints.

★ Panel or Roundtable Presentation: In a panel or roundtable discussion, you will be offering up a group of industry experts and practitioners to discuss a common challenge and how the participants were able to overcome it. Here you aren't going to tell a story (in the traditional sense of the word); instead, it will be more of a free-wheeling discussion among peers. But your session description should still adhere to the same storytelling principles already discussed to keep it compelling. You'll want to start by describing the issues to be discussed, and then highlighting a few of the topline areas the panel will cover. And if possible, close the session with a statement about what attendees will learn and what they'll be able to accomplish after hearing this dynamic talk. For an example of a panel session description, see page 112 in Resources and Helpful Hints.

★ Professional Development: Because most conferences gear their speaking agenda to be primarily educational in nature, offering a presentation directed at the professional development of attendees may be a perfect fit. Such sessions tend to be focused on the individual attendees and therefore the presentations can take on a more personal tone. The session submission can reflect this tone as well. Once again, crafting the session as a story is the best approach. For instance, if the proposed session is about how to market your own skills within an organization for your own professional advancement, you might start by describing the challenges of being noticed in a fast-paced, demanding workplace. Then describe the steps audience members can take to better market themselves by highlighting results delivered for the business. In this type of session, it's important to enumerate the lessons attendees will learn and how you will bring value to the audience. For an example of a professional development session description, see page 113 in Resources and Helpful Hints.

★ Industry Update: If you plan to provide an industry update, you can still have your submission description conform to the storytelling approach. You might start by offering some brief industry trends or regulatory issues that make your topic compelling to the audience. Then delve into the areas you'll be exploring and why the audience will be interested in hearing your perspective. If you have unique expertise on the topic, or are co-presenting with others who do, you'll want to mention that in the description. Again, wrap up the session description with a summary of what attendees will take away and why this is a must-see presentation. For an example of an industry update session description, see page 114 in Resources and Helpful Hints.

It Takes Two (or More) to Tango: How to Incorporate a Co-Presenter

There are many instances when you may feel having a co-presenter (or co-presenters) will offer a stronger session. Take for instance a case study/best-practice session. If your company is a service or solution provider, you'll want to recruit a client who has achieved tremendous success with your help to be your co-presenter. In fact, in most cases, the conference is really going to be interested in what your client has to say, as they prefer to focus on practitioners. This is true for non-business topics too. For instance, if your presentation is going to cover working with families, you might consider inviting a set of parents who have benefitted from your relationship-building tools. Are you a business coach or consultant? Invite a client who grew their business with the help of your strategies.

Because most conferences shun marketing or sales pitches, having a session built around the success of a practitioner is an excellent way to tell the story of your service or solution without being overt.

PRO TIP:
TAKE A BACKSEAT TO A PRACTITIONER.

If you are a service or solution provider, be sure to co-present with a client or partner who can serve as the voice of the practitioner. Make sure they are front and center of your session, thus demonstrating this won't be a sales or marketing pitch. Your role will be to provide additional perspective on how the success story was achieved. You may not have a leading role, but you'll still reap the considerable benefits of being associated with a winning story. And the selection committee is more likely to reward you for putting the practitioner as the face of the session.

A co-presenter should always be chosen based on the value they bring to the session. For example, if you feel your story will be enhanced and validated by the perspective of a third-party analyst or respected industry journalist, consider adding them to your session. To really grab attention and wow the conference, think outside the box when finding co-presenters. Imagine the type of attendance your HR talk on organizational development would garner if you included a retired CEO, founder of a start-up, or a leadership consultant on your panel to discuss how to nurture professional leadership.

Remember, the selection committee is typically looking for the broadest range of viewpoints and will favor those sessions that provide several perspectives on an important topic. It's worth noting that while not all presenters can be from marque-type organizations, selection committees tend to favor the big names for their agenda. After all, having presenters from Coca-Cola, Google, Harvard Business School, or the Mayo Clinic do tend to attract the most attention. However, this is not to say that lesser-known participants shouldn't even bother. On the contrary, this is why it's critically important to make sure your session description truly sings so you can compete with the big boys and girls.

Sweat the Small Stuff: Take Every Opportunity to Bolster Your Submission

In addition to the primary information gathered in the title and session description sections, some conferences will ask for some additional background materials. For instance, you might be asked to provide a list of take-aways or learning objectives. Don't treat these as an afterthought or throwaway items. You might be tempted to assume that your session description pretty much says it all, so these bonus areas are

incidental and as such don't warrant much thought. While you're probably always correct in your assessments, in this case, you're flat out wrong. Don't worry, we still love you.

The truth is, the conference hasn't put these sections in as nothing more than fluffy fillers or annoying time-wasters. In reality, they're offering you an opportunity to beef up and bolster your submission. Many people simply recap the main points of their presentation, but we believe you should use this space to drive home any pertinent information you couldn't fit in the body of your session description. And, remember, be sure to frame everything from the perspective of the attendee. Because these sections tend to require short bulleted answers, keep the text very concise. And the more impactful you can make them, the better. The selection committee will reward you for making a real effort to expand on the value of your session. As we like to say, don't leave any opportunity to shine on the table.

Some conferences will ask you to provide a list of materials attendees will receive at the conclusion of your session. Once again, how thoroughly you document those takeaway materials is another chance to show the selection committee just how valuable your session will be to those who attend. In addition to providing a copy of your PowerPoint presentation, you might consider offering:

- A practical case study (if applicable) demonstrating how your success was achieved.
- A checklist of steps you took to accomplish your goals.
- A score card outlining the pros and cons of process improvement methodologies.
- A list of tips, suggestions, and best practices for anyone looking to replicate your success.
- The research materials you sourced as the foundation of your success.

Naturally, you won't have to create the actual documents at the time of your session submission, but the more thought you can put into what you'll offer attendees, the stronger your overall session will appear to the selection committee.

Finally, many conferences require a biography for each of the session presenters. It might be tempting to drop in the standard, boilerplate bio that you use for everything, but the reality is, this is another opportunity to amp up your credibility with the selection committee. In addition to including your current job responsibilities and industry expertise, be sure to include any previous speaking experience. Conferences are always looking for dynamic speakers who have a track record of success. Of course, just because you haven't spoken before doesn't mean you will be passed over. When it comes to your bio, think creatively. Anything that helps you stand out from the crowd should be included. For more on creating a biography, see page 101 in Resources and Helpful Hints.

The Big Takeaways:

- **Put Your Best Foot Forward:** Create a session title that grabs attention while perfectly encapsulating what your presentation will be about.

- **Capture the Drama, and You'll Capture Attention:** Turn your submission into a mini-story, complete with drama to maximize its appeal with the selection committee. The more intriguing your submission is and the more passionate you can be on the subject matter, the better your chances of getting picked.

- **Length Matters, So Be Concise:** To meet the word limit for the session description, be economical with your words. Tell your story succinctly and with as much impact as you can.

- **Pick a Session Type That Ideally Suits Your Talk:** Most conferences offer different types of sessions, from case studies to panel discussions to industry updates. Choose the one that will allow you to best tell your story.

- **Broaden the Perspective of Your Presentation:** Including a co-presenter can strengthen a submission by putting a practitioner front and center for your talk. The wider the reach of your presentation, the more likely it will stand out.

- **Pay Attention to the Smallest of Details:** The session title and description are undoubtedly the most important items for a submission, but smaller details such as a list of takeaways, learning objectives, and speaker biographies are invaluable opportunities to provide further proof that your presentation is worthy of selection.

CHAPTER 5:

CRAFTING A GREAT PRESENTATION

"The best way to sound like you know what you're talking about is to know what you're talking about."

—Unknown

Congratulations! You've Been Picked to Speak: Now What?

All that hard work creating an irresistible speaker submission has finally paid off and you've just been notified that your topic has been selected for the conference. Congratulations, you've been picked! Of course, now comes the hard part. You'll need to create a presentation that lives up to the lofty promise of your proposal, which is no easy feat. However, there's no need to worry. We won't abandon you in your hour of need. The truth is that creating a memorable presentation isn't rocket science...if you know what you're doing.

In this chapter, we'll share some basic guidelines for developing a clean, compelling presentation that will engage your audience and earn favorable reviews. If you are drafting this presentation for yourself, you may suddenly be faced with the realization that you'll actually have to speak in front of hundreds of people. For some, this ignites their worst public-speaking fears. And let's be honest: no one wants to end up with rivers of sweat like Albert Brooks's anchorman character in *Broadcast News*.[5]

Even if you're an accomplished speaker who doesn't bat an eye at talking in front of a crowd, you'll still need to ensure your presentation is the best it can be. Don't forget, conferences frequently grade presenters and then factor that rating into determining who they'll invite back the following year.

In many cases, the people developing the presentation are not the same folks who will be doing the actual presenting. Marketing, public relations, and communications professionals often handle the preparation responsibilities. But regardless of whether you're a ghostwriter or a hands-on speaker, the same principles apply.

Create an Outline: The Roadmap for Your Presentation

If the subject of your presentation is extremely familiar to you—perhaps you've even given this talk a gazillion times in the past—then pulling together your speaking points won't be a challenge. However, that doesn't mean you shouldn't take this opportunity to improve on your storytelling skills.

On the other hand, if this topic is brand new to you, then spending some time organizing the key points of your talk is crucial. It may seem intuitive, but outlining your presentation is a crucial first step. Many people skip the outline because they feel they already have a good enough grasp of the topic, so why bother? The

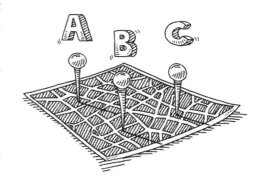

outline is important because it allows you to lay out the story in the most logical and understandable way. It also gives you perspective on how you might tell your story in the most interesting way. Think of this as the roadmap to your presentation—that includes some scenic rest stops where people will marvel at what you're saying. And much like the insistent spouse who implores you to ask for directions because you're clearly lost, we urge you to use this step to develop a clear storyline that attendees will be able to follow.

The place to start when creating your outline is your abstract. After all, it does offer a blueprint of your presentation in broad strokes. These are the bare bones of your talk. From here, you can continue to layer on details to begin developing some real depth to your talk.

PRO TIP:
START WITH WHAT MATTERS THE MOST.

In developing your outline, jot down the most important key points first. What were the biggest obstacles you faced? What unique steps did you take to overcome them? What was the big payoff or accomplishment you achieved? These will be the pillars that support your presentation.

Think Story: Engage Your Audience

We've all heard the expression: a picture is worth a thousand words. This may be true, but when it comes to a presentation, a good story is what you're aiming for. Stories are the best way to get your audience to connect with your topic and remember what you've said.

Unfortunately, this simple bit of wisdom is frequently ignored in favor of Power-Point presentation slides so crammed with statistics that they're barely readable. Don't get us wrong, powerful stats absolutely have their place in a good presentation, but stuffing them in like a turducken will more than likely overwhelm your audience and quite possi-

bly cause them to lose attention. Presentation experts and authors, Chip and Dan Heath, have conducted some revealing research on this topic. They found that after a presentation, 63 percent of attendees remembered stories, while only 5 percent remembered statistics.[6]

Turning your presentation into an engaging story is critical. At this point, you might be saying, *That's all well and good, but what exactly is a story and how do I turn my presentation into one?*

We all know a story when we hear one. But turning work-related scenarios into stories isn't necessarily easy. Luckily, the principles behind crafting a business story aren't terribly complicated, which means they can be applied by all of us.

What's Your Story? Four Steps for Turning Your Presentation into a Narrative

As mentioned earlier, story is a simple concept: "a narrative about a character overcoming some obstacle to achieve some important goal." Of course, not all presentations have a built-in story to tell. For instance, if you're talking about trends or describing a process, technique, or methodology, there might not be an apparent obstacle or even an outcome. Believe it or not, even these kinds of presentations will still benefit from the story techniques that follow. *(For the purpose of illustrating these steps, we've include a hypothetical presentation about consumer food trends in the food manufacturing industry.)*

1) Pick a hero for your story

To engage attendees, your presentation should be told from the perspective of someone they can relate to, such as you, your team, your client / customers, or even the audience themselves. This will humanize your story.

The perspective you pick will be the "good guy / gal" who attendees can root for as they overcome impediments on their journey to success. It doesn't have to be a superhero, but the bigger the challenge, the more super your everyday hero will appear. Eat your heart out, Clark Kent!

In our presentation on food trends, a logical perspective might be that of a consumer. As you develop your talk, start by considering how each of the trends you're going to discuss impacts our hero.

Instead of saying, "Our research shows that 65 percent of consumers prefer more healthful snack choices," find a story to get you there. Perhaps an anecdote where our hero (Terry) is concerned about what her kids eat because she was very unhealthy as a young child herself. This is why Terry has begun to keep only low-sodium, low-sugar, whole-grain snacks in the house.

2) Describe the hurdles

Your story should start with the challenge you, your colleagues, or your clients faced. The hero you've chosen doesn't necessarily have to be facing this challenge, but will no doubt be impacted by it.

The fact that you had to rise above a problem heightens the drama of your story and pulls listeners in. The more difficult and daunting your challenge, the more interested the audience will be in hearing how you prevailed. There's something innate in all of us that roots for people to beat the odds and succeed. This is why stories about the underdog succeeding in the face of insurmountable difficulties are so incredibly popular.

Remember, the pain point, challenge, or "bad guy/antagonist" that kicks off your story doesn't have to be central to what you ultimately accomplished. It need only describe your starting point. For instance, if you had to convince your intransigent boss that a problem existed when no one else recognized it, this could be the beginning of your story. Keep in mind, by sharing the human/emotional aspect of your challenge, you allow your audience to relate. It doesn't matter if they have had a similar problem or not. If the emotion is universal, then they'll immediately share your pain.

The food manufacturing industry faces a significant challenge due to declining sales of established brands, as Terry and others like her have begun to shift purchases to new healthier choices. Framing the industry's dilemma as a sink-or-swim turning point creates drama for your story. Will established businesses be able to pivot to meet this new demand? Or will titans fall by the wayside as consumer tastes change?

PRO TIP:
USE PERSONAL ANECDOTES TO LIVEN UP STATISTICS.

To keep statistics from being drier than a sponge in the Sahara desert, try using personal anecdotes to help illustrate the human point behind the numbers. Think of them like mini-stories in your presentation.

---

3) Reveal how tragedy turned into triumph

Tragedy might be overstating things a bit, but it does highlight that you should be thinking more dramatically in telling your story. Let's be honest, hyperbole never hurt a good story. Once you've described the challenge, now is the time to reveal how you (or the hero) were empowered to take action and overcome adversity. In its simplest terms, this is where the good guy faces off against evil and triumphs. Sticking with the hero metaphor, it's how you ended up slaying the dragon.

In this portion of your presentation, you'll want to share the lessons you took to be successful. Using business jargon, these are your best practices.

Terry and likeminded consumers have literally changed the face of the food manufacturing industry through their wallets. As a result of shifting consumer preferences, the industry as a whole is transforming to meet this new demand. In our story, you can show how this is a win-win, with Terry getting healthier snack foods she can feel good about serving to her family. And the food manufacturers are being spurred to reinvigorate venerated brands with new formulas and new ingredients that are in turn attracting greater market share than ever before.

4) Show 'em what victory looks like

The conclusion of your story is the happy ending. This is where, after having overcome insurmountable obstacles, you get to revel in your (or the hero's) accomplishments. This is the fun stuff, so make sure to give this part of your story its due.

Once again, the more you can personalize accomplishments through anecdotes, and the more you can reveal the emotion behind the success, the more your audience will connect with your story. Another important thing to keep in mind is that you want to hand the mantle over to your audience so they now have the tools to become a hero in their own right. Be sure to clearly outline the steps you took in achieving your goals.

> *Using a few choice statistics to show how food trends are expected to change over the next five years, we can make the argument that the industry is steadily becoming more attuned to Terry's likes and dislikes, and becoming more adept at identifying new trends, and then getting out ahead of them. This means, Terry is now far more trusting of her favorite brands because she is convinced manufacturers are listening to what consumers want. The story concludes by painting a rosy future for the industry.*

Hot Starts, Grabbers, and Transitions—Oh My!

In today's world of presentations, PowerPoint has become ubiquitous. Unfortunately, many people use this handy visual tool as a crutch, which actually can detract from a presentation rather than support it. The following are some simple tips for making sure your PPT presentation is working for you and not against you.

Hot starts:

After your obligatory title slide, you should have what we like to call the *hot start*. Think of this slide as your introduction to the audience. Here's your opportunity to create a positive first impression. After all, most, if not all, of these people probably have never heard you speak before, so they are getting ready to judge you and your presentation. You want the words you say in your first fifteen to twenty seconds to be surprising, dramatic, and provocative. It should also reflect your personality. First and foremost, it should draw your attendees' attention away from the millions of other things they've been thinking about prior to the start of your presentation and help them focus on your session. Keep in mind, a hot start shouldn't simply be an attention-grabbing non sequitur, but instead should set the stage for your talk. Hot starts can be an eye-popping statistic, a contrarian statement the audience wouldn't expect, it could be about a current event, a surprising trend, an un-expected result, a personal story, or a topic that's trending on social media—as long as it segues beautifully to your topic.

Grabbers:

Keeping your audiences' attention throughout your presenta-tion is critical. Perhaps you're a scintillating speaker, which will make this job much easier, but not everyone is as adept at com-manding the full focus of the audience, especially when they're tempted to check text messages, email, and the latest sports scores on our ever-intrusive smartphones. That's why we recommend that you create a grabber to introduce each major section of your pre-sentation. A grabber can be a compelling statistic, a dramatic fact, or an evocative image that ties directly to the topic you're broach-ing. Think of this as a great opening line for this part of your dis-cussion. You want to pique their interest and whet their appetites. The bolder and more interesting you can be with your grabbers, the better the chances that those smartphones will remain buried deep in your audience's pockets.

Transitions:

One of the toughest parts of the presentation for many present-ers is finding a way to move smoothly from one slide to the next. You may very well have a great story to tell for each of your slides, but if you can't transition seamlessly to the next topic, then your mojo may get derailed. And there's nothing messier than derailed mojo. A simple way to solve this problem is to develop a transi-tion sentence that you can use that will carry you to the next slide.

You may not be scripting out your entire presentation—instead using bullet points to guide your discussion—but consider scripting one sentence at the end of each slide that will help you get to the next topic. (This sentence should be on the notes section of your deck, and not the slide itself.) This type of transition could be a brief teaser setting up the next slide, or it could be a quick declarative statement on why what comes next makes a real difference in your story. Regardless, having something already scripted out will allow you to eliminate the typical "and on the next slide, we will talk about..." so you can effortlessly move from topic to topic. Your mojo will thank you!

Avoiding Death by PowerPoint

The vast majority of presentations utilize PowerPoint completely wrong. Instead of offering the audience a few visual cues that highlight the discussion, they try to cram every single detail onto each slide. We like to call this "death by PowerPoint." Comedian Don McMillan does a hilarious routine on the misuse of PowerPoint slides in a typical corporate presentation in his YouTube video, "Life After Death By PowerPoint."[7] The point is, don't use your slides as notes for your talk. That's what the notes section of your deck is for. Or if you prefer, you can create a separate printout. Your slides should have a minimal amount of text that is very easy to read (translation: clean, big font size). Remember to keep your audience in mind when building your slides. You certainly want them to have something to look at, but at the same time, you don't want to distract them from what's really important—you!

Now in many cases, your PowerPoint deck will also be distributed to the attendees as a takeaway. You may be thinking, *I have to fit everything on the slides, so the audience will be able to fully understand the story of my presentation when they look at the deck later.* This does present a bit of a dilemma. If you follow our advice and only include succinct phrases highlighting key points in the slide text, much of your presentation will not be included with the takeaway. Some conferences will allow you to provide a separate deck or printout that contains a much deeper dive for distribution to attendees who are interested. If this isn't possible, you'll want to strike a balance, keeping the text on your slides to a minimum, while still fully telling your story.

Appeal to the Eye:
Visual Style Counts

There are lots of different philosophies when it comes to the visual style of the PPT slides used in support of a presentation. Some conferences will have some basic guidelines about what you can and cannot include, such as the use of your company logo or product glamour shots. Some will provide a template that you will be expected to utilize. This is typically done to ensure all the presenters' decks at the conference have a somewhat uniform graphical look. More often than not, you will be left to your own devices when it comes to deciding what belongs on the pages of your deck. Fancy is not necessary, but you certainly want your slides to have a clean look. As a good rule of thumb, ensure you leave a liberal amount of open, white space between lines of text and around images. This allows the audience to easily scan the slide without being overwhelmed. Again, you really want the primary focus to be on you, the speaker, and not some cluttered PowerPoint slides.

PRO TIP:
IGNORE STANDARDIZED TEMPLATES AT YOUR PERIL.

It's tempting to ignore the standardized template the conference has instructed you to use because you've got a much cooler one in mind. Bad idea. Nothing annoys the organizers more than someone who thinks they're above the rules. Chances are pretty good, if you don't follow the guidelines, you won't be invited back.

Every Picture Tells a Story, Don't It?

Pretty safe bet Rod Stewart wasn't offering advice about PowerPoint slides when he penned those famous lyrics, "Every picture tells a story, don't it?"[8] But it turns out to be good advice nonetheless. Thank you, Rod!

It's tempting to simply bullet-point the information on your slides, creating a data-heavy companion in support of your discussion. However, pictures have been scientifically proven to be far more effective in conveying information. Research has shown the brain is able to process pictures much faster than words. In fact, neuroscientists at MIT found the brain can identify images in as little as thirteen milliseconds.[9]

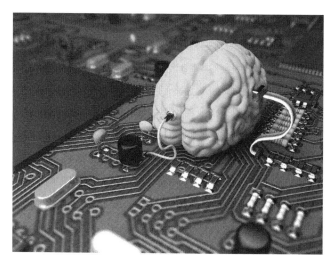

This explains why people tend to respond better to visual information than plain text. After all, our brains are essentially just a computer—albeit a really squishy, gray-matter-powered computer. And apparently one that likes pictures and graphics; so try to use evocative images wherever possible to communicate key points. Apparently, Rod Stewart knew what he was talking about.

Wrapping Up Your Presentation and Other Assorted Suggestions

Now that you've gotten this far, you have basically done all the heavy lifting. Take a moment and pat yourself on the back. However, before you do your happy dance, we have a few additional suggestions we'd like to share to help you squeeze every drop of excellence from your presentation.

Recap:

After you've finished telling your story, it's always a good idea to recap the lessons learned. This is your opportunity to drive home any best practices you've accumulated along your journey to success. This is what your audience is truly interested in hearing. They want to learn how you did it so they can replicate your success. It's also a nice way to summarize what your session has been all about.

Q&A:

Most conferences require that you reserve some time at the end of your session for an audience question-and-answer period. Attendees have been attentively listening to you speak, and now it's their turn to share an opinion, ask further questions, or offer their own perspective. A lively Q&A is the sign that your presentation has intrigued your audience to the point that they want to know more.

Of course, sometimes getting things rolling can be difficult. It's kind of like being back in grade school. No one wants to be the first one to raise their hand. So, just in case this happens to you, we recommend that you prepare a few questions of your own in advance. You can either seed these questions in the audience with friends or colleagues, who then ask them during the Q&A, or you can simply break the ice yourself. Once you've opened the floor up to questions, if no one seems to be chiming in, just say something like, "A couple of you were talking to me prior to this presentation and asked…" or "A question I frequently get when talking to folks about what we did…" or "Here's a question that might be on many of your minds…" Before you know it, the audience will join in on the fun.

Contact info:

This may seem rudimentary, but don't forget to include a slide with your contact information on it. Because your deck will in all likelihood also be a leave-behind for attendees, it is imperative that you include a way for them to get in touch. Whether it's for networking purposes, to develop possible leads for your organization, or just to hear from an adoring public, you'll want to include a contact slide.

Divide and conquer:

If you're working with a co-presenter, you'll want to choreograph how you're going to divide up the presentation well before you put your deck together. Bear in mind, you should carefully consider what is the best way to tell your respective sides to the story, so the overall presentation will deliver the greatest value from an attendee perspective. Whatever you do, avoid being redundant.

Slide count:

A question we frequently get is, how many slides do I need for my presentation? There's no strict rule on this, but we go with one slide for every one to two minutes of your presentation. So, if you're speaking for forty-five minutes, you'll want approximately twenty to thirty slides. Obviously, you may choose to use more slides or fewer slides depending on your own presentation style. But whatever you decide, try not to overcomplicate things by having too many slides. It will only distract your audience and detract from your session. In the end, the most important thing is how well you tell your story. The most beautiful PowerPoint deck in the world won't make a bit of difference if your story is a dud.

The Big Takeaways:

- ☐ **An Outline Will Keep You in Line:** Start drafting your presentation by first outlining your talk. List the key points and then expand on these to create a logical progression that best tells your success story.

- ☐ **Grab Your Audience by the Ears:** While being informative is important, engaging your audience is key. Turning your presentation into a compelling story is critical.

- ☐ **Follow Basic Storytelling Rules:** A good story needs a hero (protagonist) and a villain (antagonist). Find the hero in your story and create a narrative from their perspective. Lead attendees through the challenges faced, and how the hero overcame all obstacles to achieve a successful outcome.

- ☐ **Wake 'Em Up:** The opening of your presentation should grab the audience's attention. Use a hot start (a provocative image or an eye-popping statistic) to kick-start your talk.

- ☐ **Keep Them on the Edge of Their Seats:** Start each major section of your talk with a compelling statistic, a dramatic fact, or an evocative statement. This will pique your audience's interest and keep them off their smartphones.

- ☐ **Take the Angst out of Transitions:** Script a sentence in advance to help you smoothly move from each slide to the next, avoiding any awkward transitions.

- ☐ **Keep Slides Simple:** Don't try to throw everything including the kitchen sink onto your PowerPoint slides. Use a minimal amount of text, a large font, and plenty of white space to make it easy for the audience to scan quickly and stay focused on you.

- ☐ **Why Use Words When a Picture Will Do:** Pictures and graphics are far easier for the audience to scan and digest, so use images on your slides wherever possible to convey themes and ideas.

CHAPTER 6:

RESOURCES AND HELPFUL HINTS

"The journey of a thousand miles begins with one step."
—Lao Tzu

Other Stuff We Know You'll Need

After years of working on speaker proposals, we've assembled an assorted compendium of information that has helped us be successful. What you'll find on the following pages is a collection of tips, dos and don'ts, and other tidbits that we know you'll need to achieve your own success. Consider these resource tools your cheat sheets!

After Giving Your Presentation, What's Next?

The conference is over and now you're basking in the afterglow of success. Or perhaps you're just relieved it went well and you didn't throw up. Either way, you deserve a hearty pat on the back for fulfilling your objective of getting picked and then giving a gangbuster presentation. This truly is no small feat, and you should take a moment to revel in your glory.

Okay, that's enough.

Perhaps you're thinking, *Now that the conference is over, my work here is done.* Wrong! If you're enterprising, there are lots of ways you can squeeze additional mileage out of the hard work you put in to creating your speaker proposal and presentation.

A Simple Thank-You Goes a Long Way

Your first post-conference step should be to send thank-you notes to anyone who was involved in making your presentation possible. You might consider issuing a simple thank-you to colleagues and senior managers, as well as the conference organizers. If you received any inquiries from attendees, you should follow up with a thank-you for attending your session. This small, but all-too-frequently forgotten, bit of social etiquette can go a long way toward ingratiating you for the future.

Repurpose Content to Your Heart's Content

The content you created for your presentation needn't be relegated to the dustbin following the conference. There are several ways you can repurpose your presentation and get more mileage out of it. One way is to simply create an article or blog post based on the topic of your talk. You can publish this yourself on your personal blog, or other social media sites such as LinkedIn, or submit to a trade publication in your industry. If your organization has an intranet site, you might consider offering the article up for publication there.

Another good use for your content is to essentially recreate your talk in the form of a webinar that you can then offer to your customers through your website or other social media outlets such as Blab.im. Repurposing the content in this way is simple to do since you already have the entire presentation worked out. This is an excellent way to extend your thought leadership.

Also consider posting your presentation deck on SlideShare. net. It's a repository for presentations and it's a great way to extend your knowledge and message to an audience beyond your live session.

Refresh Your Topic for Submission to Other Conferences

Most conferences require that your speaker proposal be original. But there's certainly nothing stopping you from modifying your existing proposal a bit and submitting it elsewhere. If it was picked once, there's a good chance the topic will attract the attention of another conference. Don't forget, you'll want to tailor your proposal to the specific focus and audience of the new conference.

And the Winner Is...

Your dynamic speaker proposal and presentation can make the basis for an excellent award submission. Clearly, you've accomplished a lot, which is why your presentation was chosen in the first place. Why not repurpose the content for consideration for an award in your industry?

Research awards the same way you looked for conferences—Google search and identify award programs that are a fit, draft your nomination in accordance with the rules, and meet the deadlines. You just might end up with some trophy-case-worthy hardware in addition to your speaking accolades!

"Great geniuses have the shortest biographies."
—Ralph Waldo Emerson

A Few Brief Words on How to Write a Short Bio

Most speaker submissions require the inclusion of a short biography on each of the presenters. As mentioned previously, this isn't a throwaway item. Think of the bio as another opportunity to lay out your bona fides and hopefully further impress the selection committee.

Because the word limit for bios is typically short, sometimes as few as fifty or sixty words, it's important to include only what is essential. Admittedly, summarizing your qualifications in just a handful of sentences isn't easy. Once again, consider your audience. Ask yourself: What do attendees need to know about me, the speaker, in order to decide if they want to spend an hour or more of their precious time locked in a room with me?

The primary focus of the bio should be to outline your professional accomplishments as they relate to the topic of your talk. While highlights of your life and career, including all previously held jobs, might be scintillating, you probably won't have room for a complete résumé. It's important to include expertise and accomplishments that qualify you to speak on your chosen topic.

Me, Myself, and I: Which Person Is Best?

One of the most frequently asked questions we get is: What person should the bio be written in? Should it be first person ("I am a third-grade teacher.") or third person ("Eileen is a vice president.")? And should first names be used as opposed to the more formal surnames?

In the past, bios tended to be written in third person and used only surnames. But those stodgy old standards have given way to a more flexible approach. For most speaker submissions, you'll probably want to keep things professional, sticking to the third person, but using first names throughout the bio will give a more approachable feel to it.

Speaking Experience a Plus

As mentioned earlier in this book, be sure to include any speaking experience in your bio. Selection committees always look favorably on speakers with a proven track record. The fact that you've spoken before is proof you have what it takes. (Actually, it just means you were picked, but presumably your prior experience will serve you well.) Previous speaking experience adds to your credibility and improves your odds of being selected. Even if you haven't spoken at a conference before but have participated in seminars, webinars, or other formal events, be sure to include these in your bio.

Don't worry if you haven't spoken publicly in the past—this won't diminish your chances. After all, if you have a great topic and solid submission, the selection committee will be more than likely to give you the nod of approval.

What Else Should I Say about Myself?

Still struggling with what to include in your bio? Use this questionnaire to help you draw out some additional facts about yourself. Answer these questions and use the details to compose your bio:

- What is your job title?
- What are your job responsibilities?
- What three positions did you hold prior to your current position (include company names and job titles)? Please briefly describe your responsibilities.
- Do you have any industry certifications (e.g., CFP, CPA, etc.)?
- Are you a member of any industry or community organizations?
- Have you spoken at any major conferences or trade associations? If so, which ones, when, and what were the topics?
- Where did you go to college? In what subject did you earn your degree? Did you earn any advanced degrees?
- Is there anything else you'd like to share?

Fill-in-the-Blank Bio Template

The following is a generic template you can use to create a short but highly effective bio:

_____ _____ is a _____
(first name) (last name)   (job title)

for _____. He/she is responsible for
        (employer)

_____. Under _____'s
        (list major job responsibilities)   (first name)

leadership, _____.
                    (list significant accomplishments or milestones for the organization)

With _____ years of experience in the industry, he/she
        (# of years)

_____. _____ is a
        (list knowledge of industry and/or marketplace)   (first name)

_____. He/she has
        (list professional designations, accreditations, or certifications)

been recognized by _____.
                            (include industry, organization, or peer awards or regocnition)

_____ is a highly sought-after speaker, having
(first name)

presented at _____.
                    (list previous speaking engagements)

Questions to Ask Yourself When Preparing Your Session Description

Every good speaker proposal starts with explaining how you are going to answer your audience's most pressing questions.

Here's a list of questions that will help you define the key points you will use to create your session description for your speaker proposal. Remember that your proposed session will likely be in competition with similar topics from other potential presenters so make sure yours is well-defined and compelling! Answering these questions can help you identify the most important points of your topic so you can make sure they stand out in your final proposal.

Questions for a Case Study Proposal

- What was the problem that was plaguing your organization/team that moved you to seek a solution?

- What process did you undertake to develop the solution you used? Was the process unique to your job function or industry?

- What plan did you develop to implement your solution?

- Who was involved in the implementation? Did other departments or teams participate?

- Did you encounter any unanticipated problems that required a creative solution?

- How long did it take to implement your solution? Did you have a tight timeline? Were other deadlines in play that made your implementation unique?

- What were the results of your solution? Did you achieve your goals? What did you use to measure your outcomes?

- What will attendees of your presentation learn by attending your presentation?

- What learning objectives do you have for your attendees?

- Are there any knowledge prerequisites the audience should have?

- What are the two or three most important things you want the audience to walk away knowing after they attend your presentation?

Questions for an Industry or Topical Trend Proposal

- What is driving the shift in current trends?
- How are current trends impacting the way you and your peers conduct business or execute their special interest?
- How is the industry/group responding to these changing trends?
- What solutions or work-arounds are industry professionals/participants using to manage the impact of the trend shifts?
- What are industry analysts/topical experts predicting about where trends are headed?
- What response do professionals/participants need or want to see from industry regulators or industry participants?
- What guidance can you offer to your peers for how to best manage the current industry climate?
- What are the two or three most important things you want your audience to learn about this trend by attending your presentation?

Question for a Roundtable Discussion Proposal

- What are the common issues you face as a group? How do these issues reflect what your industry/area of interest peers are facing?
- What are the most pressing questions your peer group has about this topic?
- How do you individually address these issues?
- Who are some leading industry observers that could participate in your panel to provide third-party perspective?
- What two or three things will your audience learn from your collective discussion of this topic?

Dos and Don'ts

Need a little direction on what you need to do to get your speaker proposal picked? Take a look here for some help on important things to remember when pitching a conference (and once you've landed a speaking spot) and tips on making your session shine.

Looking for Conferences

Do start researching call-for-speaker deadlines ten to twelve months in advance of the actual conference event.

Don't be discouraged if you've missed the call-for-speaker's window. Make a note of when the conference accepts proposals and plan to submit for the following year.

Do include local and regional conferences, as well as national events on your prospect list.

Don't dismiss smaller events because of their size. Smaller audiences can pay big dividends by delivering local connections and business opportunities.

Do include conferences that are indirectly related to your field of interest to broaden your audience reach.

Do look into speaking at digital events like webinars and online conferences.

Do learn each conference's rules for accepting speaker proposals. Follow them to the letter.

Don't assume the conference will allow you to make changes not addressed by their proposal rules. Contact the conference in advance for guidance if you want to propose something unique.

Do use your personal and professional network and let them know you are looking for speaking opportunities. They can be a great source of information and referral to conference organizers.

Picking a Topic

Do pick a topic that lets you showcase your unique expertise, success story, or distinct perspective.

Don't be boring! Your topic should interest a broad range of conference attendees.

Do use your business goals or priorities as a filter when determining what topic to propose.

Do consider the latest innovations, issues, or controversies as topics.

Don't propose to speak on topics that are dated or are no longer relevant to your audience.

Writing Your Abstract

Do make sure your title is creative and describes your topic. It's the first thing the conference committee will see, so make it good!

Don't dismiss using a straightforward title for your session if a creative twist doesn't fit.

Do write your abstract from the perspective of what the audience will receive from attending your session.

Don't make your credentials, product, or service the focus of your abstract. Make it about your audience, not about you.

Do frame the problem, challenge, or issue at the start of your session description. It demonstrates you understand what your audience faces.

Don't be vague about what your session will address.

Do describe the solution you've discovered, the perspective you hold, and why it's important for your audience to know what you've learned.

Don't skimp on the specifics of what you'll share if you're selected. The conference needs to know you'll be sharing valuable content with their audience.

Creating Your Presentation Slides

Do confirm if the conference needs your deck in advance so they can load it onto an onsite computer system.

Don't sell your product in your deck. Most conferences frown on outright selling by session presenters so keep your slides focused on educating your audience.

Do start your deck by revisiting your presentation proposal. Make sure your slides deliver on what you said you would talk about.

Don't use your presentation deck as a big text document. Sparse text and compelling images will make your presentation memorable.

Do make sure your slides are available to the audience after your session. Consider creating a second deck as a handout with more details on the slides than used in your presentation.

Don't make the mistake of not proofing your slides before your session. There's nothing worse than having typos show up on a 150-foot screen!

Other Bits and Pieces

Do take advantage of every content opportunity the proposal form offers. Leave nothing blank!

Don't neglect your bio. Make sure it's well written and captures your work experience as well as your past speaking experience.

Do read your speaker's contract carefully and follow all the rules and meet all the deadlines your conference sets.

Don't forget to send a thank-you note to the conference organizer after the show, letting them know you appreciated them including you on the agenda.

Do repurpose your session description for other conferences. Make subtle changes to the content to make it fit additional conferences you plan to pitch.

Don't forget to look for opportunities to extend your message. Offer to write an article for the sponsoring organization's member publication. Or write an article based on your presentation and post it on LinkedIn.

Do consider leveraging your conference proposal for an award submission with an industry trade publication. You've already done all the heavy lifting!

*"Life is like a cup of tea...
it's all how you make it."*
—**Unknown**

A Tasty Sampler of Speaker Submissions

Speaker proposals come in all shapes and sizes. Every conference has its own criteria, which will dictate what goes into the proposal. The real challenge for submitters is getting the very most out of their submission—with the obvious hope they will *get picked* to speak.

The following are a few examples of speaker submissions for a grab bag of different types of conferences and speaking formats:

Sample #1

Conference Type: Technology

Proposal Type: Case Study

Proposal Title: Harnessing the Power of Mobile Video: The Future of Marketing Is in Our Hands

Submission Abstract:
In today's marketing universe, video may currently be king, but mobile video is poised to become the emperor. A recent Forrester survey found that one minute of video has the equivalent value of 1.8 million words, making it a potent tool for communicating a brand's message. As more and more online content is being consumed via mobile devices, marketers face new challenges in ensuring their brand messages are resonating with customers and prospects. In this session, leading national retailer, Acme Inc., will share best practices in creating an engaging viewing experience while sustaining brand consistency. We will examine how to track and quantify results across devices and formats in order to better understand how campaigns are performing. Attendees will learn about current and future trends in marketing with mobile video and how mobile web and apps can be leveraged to drive engagement, increase conversions, and build stronger brand relationships.

Sample #2

Conference Type: Social Media

Proposal Type: Panel Discussion

Proposal Title: If You Build It, They Will Buy: The Power of a Thriving Community in Fostering Brand Loyalty

Submission Abstract:

In today's highly complex world of commerce, it has become increasingly difficult for businesses to create meaningful, lasting connections with potential customers. Community offers a unique opportunity to break through the clutter. When built correctly, an engaged community can be a powerful tool for fostering critical brand loyalty. In this roundtable discussion, our panel of community experts will discuss the most important aspects of building a brand community. We will outline best practices and strategies for creating a successful community. Our panelists will share the latest trends and top community tools. Attendees will learn the primary process for growing a more committed community and practical steps for achieving positive brand connection. We will answer key questions, such as who should be invited into the community, what community guidelines should be created, how to effectively moderate a community, what it takes to encourage robust community growth, and how best to achieve vital business goals. After attending this session, the audience will come away with a far greater understanding of how to create a thriving community and driving improved brand loyalty.

Sample #3

Conference Type: Human Resources

Proposal Type: Workshop

Proposal Title: What Have You Done for Your Career Lately? The Importance of Self-Marketing

Submission Abstract:
Business is booming, and that's due in no small measure to the outstanding efforts of you and your team. However, senior management may be blissfully unaware of your many accomplishments, which means your career won't benefit from your considerable contributions to the company's success. While focused on doing their jobs, business professionals often fail to effectively market their own skills and accomplishments, instead working in relative anonymity. In this workshop, career development professionals will discuss the critical need to market successes internally to shine a spotlight on the value of your work to the company. We will outline important strategies, such as showcasing important results and work product, and leveraging social media tools to underscore accomplishments. Attendees will gain practical tips on how to use marketing principles to get the word out about what they're doing, how they're making an impact, and what it means to the organization, thus enabling them to affirm their value to the business. This is a can't-miss session for anyone looking to advance their career and achieve the recognition they deserve.

Sample #4

Conference Type: Pharmaceutical

Proposal Type: Industry Update

Proposal Title:
Avoiding Compromise When It Comes to
Preventing Compromise of the Immune System

Submission Abstract:
Rapid advancements in pharmaceutical development are
changing the face of disease treatment and prevention, putting greater emphasis on innovative immunotoxicology assessment tools to mitigate safety risks. Improving patient
health and safety is at stake as new drug development plat-
forms come to the forefront. In this presentation, our distinguished medical experts will review the latest safety trends
in pharmaceutical development. We will provide an over-
view of ICH guidelines and current paradigms in immunotoxicology. Amongst the topics to be discussed will be the
application of immunophenotyping to safety assessment;
the utility of the T-dependent antibody response as a best
practice in immunotoxicology; and the contradictory role of
cytokines as friend or foe. Attendees will also benefit from
an in-depth update on the latest regulatory mandates related to immunotoxicology and recent trends in FDA approv-
als. This is a must-attend session for anyone in the industry
looking to stay abreast of this evolving science and how patient outcomes will be impacted in the short and long-term.

Building a Speaker's Package

If you aspire to take your speaking opportunities to the next level and become a featured or keynote speaker for conference events, you'll need to build a great speaker's package. You can use your conference speaking experience as a launching pad to a speaking career that includes presenting in front of larger audiences and even getting paid to speak about your topic.

When conferences are looking for a featured or keynote speaker, they want to know as much as they can about you to see if you're a fit for their program and their audience. The best way you can share this is by creating and maintaining a speaker's package. One common method is to develop a speaker's page on a simple website, but if that's not an option for you, create a document that can be easily sent to anyone who inquires about your availability to speak.

There are lots of speaker's package examples out there, and most cover the following list of items:

- **What They Can Expect:** Explain what the conference can expect from you: responsiveness, phone or in-person meetings to understand the conference's goals and needs, your support of the event through your social media channels, a professional speaker that is focused on your audience, resources you'll make available to the audience, post-event follow-up to get feedback.

- **Bio:** This bio should be more extensive and more expansive than the bio you use for your speaker proposals. It should validate your expertise and highlight why you're passionate about your topic. Include past conferences and venues you've spoken at and the size of the audiences you've presented in front of (if relevant).

- **Video Clips:** Video clips are critical if you want to take your public speaking effort to the next level. Use your conference speaking opportunities (no matter the size!) to begin growing a library of clips and be sure to capture video as you speak in front of larger audiences.

- **Most Requested Topics:** Use this section to share your most requested speaking topics. And if you're just starting out, use this section to summarize the topics you can talk about.

- **Testimonials:** If you have testimonials from event organizers or audience members from past presentations, use them here to let interested conference planners know what others have loved about your presentations. If you don't have testimonials to share, use evaluation scores from events you have presented at previously.

- **Upcoming Engagements:** Have some speeches booked in the future? List the dates and times in this section. Be sure to include a link to the event so people can click and find it easily.

- **Previous Engagements:** List your past speaking events here. List dates, times, and links if there are any resources posted about the event.

- **Next Steps/Contact Form:** Make it easy for people to get in touch with you!

*"There are no bad words. Bad thoughts. Bad
intentions, and wooooords."*
— George Carlin

Putting Words in Your Mouth: Strong Versus Weak

Because your speaker proposal will be severely limited in its
word count, you need to make each and every one count. This
means avoiding the use of weak words and maximizing strong
ones. Strong words will provide that added punch to your copy
and help ensure you get picked to speak.

Weak Words

Weak or passive words are often seen as vague, lacking specificity, unnecessary, and not particularly confident.

You should avoid using **weak** words, such as:

- Really
- Things
- I believe
- Very
- Bad
- Nice
- Fun
- Awesome
- Cool
- Interesting
- Some
- Almost

- Enough
- Fairly
- Guess
- Just
- Looked
- Nearly
- Probably
- Seemed
- Slightly
- Sometimes
- Somewhat
- Trying

Strong Words

Strong or positive words should make the reader feel something. Carefully chosen power words can have the effect of drawing them in and connecting with the topic. Obviously, it's important not to overuse such words, but a few strategically sprinkled throughout your submission can go a long way toward strengthening your prose.

You should use **strong** words, such as:

- Absolutely
- Acclaimed
- Amazing
- Breathtaking
- Brilliant
- Complete
- Creative
- Daring
- Delight
- Devoted
- Distinguished
- Efficient
- Eye-opening
- Fulfilling
- Ingenious
- Innovative

- Jaw-dropping
- Lucrative
- Mind-blowing
- Powerful
- Productive
- Remarkable
- Revolutionary
- Sensational
- Surprising
- Smart
- Successful
- Transformative
- Unwavering
- Valued
- Visionary

Now You Know What We Know

After fifteen years of writing speaker proposals, we've seen it all—the good, the bad, and the ugly. What we've shared with you in this book is all the good, the great, and the powerful that has helped us land hundreds of speaking spots for our clients. With everything you've learned, you're ready to secure a few speaking spots for yourself. You've got all the tools you'll need to be successful.

The best way to test your new knowledge is to get out there and give it a try. We can't encourage you enough to research some events that are a fit for you and submit a speaker proposal. You'll confirm and affirm your expertise and at the same time let others in your sphere of influence learn from your deep knowledge base. There are lots of people who need to know what you know—it's time to get out there and share it with them!

We wish you nothing but success in meeting your goal of becoming a conference speaker. Great things await you. We're confident you'll see the fruits of your labors before you know it.

We would love to hear about your success. Feel free to share how things are going with your proposal efforts at our website, www.GetPickedToSpeak.com.

Aurora Gregory and David Pitlik
Los Angeles, California

ABOUT THE AUTHORS

AURORA GREGORY

As an eighth grader, Aurora was a finalist in a speech contest. She didn't win, but that just might have been the start of her career as a communicator. Some of the biggest brands in business have worked with her to get their message right, create communications programs that connect with target audiences, and set marketing strategies—all achieving stellar results. Aurora's gotten high marks as a communications trainer, helping people develop skills to deliver their most important messages to customers, media, and presentation audiences. She has years of experience in leading speaker's bureau programs that have placed hundreds of speakers at local, national, and international conferences. When she's not talking, you'll likely find her hiking the foothills in her hometown or on the sofa watching classic movies.

CONNECT WITH AURORA ON LINKEDIN
www.linkedin.com/in/auroragregory

DAVID PITLIK

David is an expert storyteller and seasoned writer who has mastered the fine art of marketing, communications, and public relations—all modesty aside. He has earned a strong reputation for his ability to transform industry and technical jargon into engaging, comprehensible language and infusing content with compelling stories for maximum impact. He has years of experience creating speaker proposals, helping hundreds of experts claim speaking spots at regional, national, and international conferences. Putting words in the mouths of clients comes easily to David, having spent seventeen years as a network television comedy writer. When he's not making his clients look good through standout ghostwriting, he earns the occasional honor for himself, such as the Los Angeles PRism Award for excellence in writing and communications, and PCLA PRo Award for best writing for an in-house corporate newsletter.

CONNECT WITH DAVID ON LINKEDIN
www.linkedin.com/in/davidpitlik

ACKNOWLEDGMENTS

If there's one thing we've learned it's that writing a book takes a village. We have had the good fortune of having a great village made up of clients, colleagues, family, and friends who have shared everything from their wisdom to much-needed cheerleading, all of which we needed in order to bring the vision of this book to life. We could not have reached our goal of creating what we know is going to be a go-to resource for anyone wanting to share their knowledge with conference audiences. We want to specifically thank the following people who have contributed so much:

Shayla Eaton of Curiouser Editing, who gave two first-time authors a great confidence boost by affirming our work and confirming its value. She is the invaluable resource every independent author should have to make sure the hard work they've put in gets presented to the world in the best possible way.

Lena Elizer of Lena Elizer Designs, who created our book cover and web site. She gave *Get Picked* the visual branding we needed to drive our message home. Her work was the first tangible "thing" developed for the book and we love the look now just as much as we did when we saw it for the first time.

James Woosley of Free Agent Press, who designed the layout for both the ebook and print editions of *Get Picked*. James masterfully dealt with some unique design challenges in the book, giving us options to consider and his recommendations for how to make this book look as good as it reads. His creativity, responsiveness, and thoughtful attention to detail made sure we presented the very best to the world with our first book.

Karyn Giss, David's wife, who has offered unwavering encouragement, loving support, and countless meals to feed his growling stomach after long days of writing.

Daniel Pitlik, David's brother, who has provided invaluable counsel and brilliant feedback during the drafting of several chapters. Daniel's wisdom in the art of presenting has been the inspiration for many key concepts in this book.

Ken Carlton, writer extraordinaire and great friend, who gave freely of his self-publishing expertise and continues to serve as a role model for pursuing one's dreams.

Kenneth Gregory, Aurora's husband, who has tirelessly cheered on this effort and who has never missed a chance to promote the book and even wrote a brilliant, creative, one-page summary of the content.

Angel and Dwayne Cantrell, Aurora's brother and sister, who celebrated every milestone of the book-writing and publishing process. Their moral support was and is so encouraging and motivating.

Aleacia Widdows, Aurora's #hillkiller friend, who, during early-morning walks up very steep hills, never lost confidence that this book would become a reality.

Eileen Zicchino, a wonderful client who has become a wonderful friend. Her validation of our idea to write this book gave us the confidence we needed to move forward. She also promised to create a gang sign for the book and once she did that, we knew we had to write it.

Patrick Moore, who has hired us every chance he could no matter where he worked. The genesis of the strategies we use were developed working for Patrick and it was working with him that we earned our first success.

The Association for Financial Professionals and specifically John Gibson and Casey Breslin for allowing us to share our content with your audience. We appreciate your confidence and your support.

Mary Ellen Saunders, who, as a seasoned association executive, allowed us over the years to gain deep understanding of what conferences want to present to their attendees and never missed an opportunity to praise our work.

The hundreds of conference speaker hopefuls that have entrusted us with their proposals and taken our counsel. Every time you let us work with you, you validate our strategies. We would not know what we know without you.

Special thanks to everyone who has taken the time to offer us advice, kind words, and great suggestions.

And finally, thanks to Omar, whose constant badgering to deliver beyond expectations has inspired us to be our best selves.

—**Aurora & David**

SOURCES

1. Hannah Morgan, Undercover Recruiter, "15 LinkedIn Status Updates to Get You Noticed." Accessed March 11, 2016. http://theundercoverrecruiter.com/linkedin-updates-get-noticed/.

2. Wikipedia, "The Most Interesting Man in the World." Accessed March 17, 2016. https://en.wikipedia.org/wiki/The_Most_Interesting_Man_in_the_World.

3. Kendall Haven, *Story Proof: The Science Behind the Startling Touch of Story* (Libraries Unlimited: 2007).

4. U.S. PIRG, "21st Century Transportation." Accessed April 25, 2016. http://www.uspirg.org/reports/usp/new-direction.

5. *Broadcast News*, "Aaron Struggles on Air." Accessed April 25, 2016. https://www.youtube.com/watch?v=A5xTu6AMxq4.

6. Dan and Chip Heath, *Made to Stick: Why Some Ideas Survive and Others Die* (Random House: 2007).

7. Don McMillan, "Life after Death by PowerPoint." Accessed April 25, 2016. https://www.youtube.com/watch?v=lpvgfmEU2Ck.

8. Rod Stewart, "Every Picture Tells a Story." Accessed April 25, 2016. https://www.youtube.com/watch?v=T9GapvypdEo.

9. Anne Trafton, MIT News, "In the Blink of An Eye." Accessed April 25, 2016. http://news.mit.edu/2014/in-the-blink-of-an-eye-0116.

Need more guidance on creating irresistible speaker proposals?

Landed a speaking spot at a conference using our tips, tricks, and tools?

Interested in having us work with your team on building a conference speaker's bureau campaign?

We want to hear from you!

Contact us at our website:

WWW.GETPICKEDTOSPEAK.COM

Made in the USA
San Bernardino, CA
12 July 2017